SKIING
The Mind Game

Other Dell Books available from
Marlin M. Mackenzie

TENNIS: THE MIND GAME
GOLF: THE MIND GAME

SKIING

The Mind Game

Marlin M. Mackenzie, Ed.D., with Ken Denlinger

A DELL TRADE PAPERBACK

A DELL TRADE PAPERBACK

Published by
Dell Publishing
a division of
Bantam Doubleday Dell Publishing Group, Inc.
1540 Broadway
New York, New York 10036

Library of Congress Cataloging in Publication Data

Mackenzie, Marlin M.
    Skiing : the mind game / Marlin M. Mackenzie with Ken
Denlinger.
        p.   cm.
    Includes index.
    ISBN 0-440-50457-0
    1. Skis and skiing—Psychological aspects.   I. Denlinger, Ken.
II. Title.
GV854.9.P75M33   1993
796.93—dc20   93-20387
                                                                      CIP

Printed in the United States of America

Published simultaneously in Canada

November 1993

10 9 8 7 6 5 4 3 2 1
BVG

CONTENTS

ACKNOWLEDGMENTS

Lots of people shared directly and indirectly in the development of this book and the two before it, *Golf: The Mind Game* and *Tennis: The Mind Game*. They were athletes from many different sports, my students, my collaborating author, my agent, and most of all my wife, Edna.

A dozen or so outstanding skiers were exceedingly helpful because they allowed me to rummage around in their brains to find out how their minds work, especially with regard to how they managed fear. And they validated my techniques when they actually performed better after using them.

My graduate students at Teachers College, Columbia University, constantly challenged me while I was training them to become sports counselors. Their analytical minds and healthy skepticism enabled me to refine and expand my techniques.

My collaborator, Ken Denlinger, continued to help and encourage me to make the book clear and readable.

My agent, Faith Hamlin, had the insight and confidence to recognize that my earliest draft of a book for athletes in general contained the seeds of a publishable book; and she obviously convinced others to agree with her.

Edna, my wife and companion, deserves a hearty hug and immeasurable thanks for her emotional support and patience as I struggled alone to edit this third book. Her hours of editing the first two books taught me how to polish this one.

To all of these people I say, "Thanks!"

MMM
Rio Verde, Arizona
April 1993

INTRODUCTION

People pay dearly to ski. They wear expensive, colorful clothing to keep from being frostbitten, and bind equally expensive sliding boards to stiff, foam-filled boots for schussing down the mountain. The cost of all this gear can amount to more than two thousand dollars. They also pay a small fortune to fly to slopes in Colorado, Vermont, Switzerland, and other out-of-the way mountains. They rent condos fit for royalty and buy daily lift tickets that equal the *prix fixe* cost of luncheon at Le Cirque. At these prices, skiing is not just a recreational pastime but it becomes a costly investment as well.

What's more, skiers—novice or expert—live on the edge of danger, risking injury on the lifts to the top of the hill and on each run to the bottom. Novices mince their way haltingly to the base of a bunny run with muscles tighter than Robin Hood's bowstring. Many intermediates and experts attack the mountain with bravado, like squirrels leaping from limb to limb, risking injury to a limb or two of their own, and to others on the hill.

Yet nearly all skiers, in expensive, dogged, and often reckless pursuit of the perfect run and enjoyment of *après*-ski affairs, rarely invest any thought to what will help them ski proficiently.

Their own minds.

I propose to change that. In this book I explain the ways in which your mind, more marvelous than any computer, can be tapped to manage fear and improve your skiing. Wouldn't you want to experience rhythmical, carved turns and exquisite control of your skis rather than the anxious or fearful moments when you struggle to maintain your balance?

What I offer is a practical, down-to-earth system that uses the mind and emotions to regulate skiing—and this system *works,* whether you are a World Cup professional, a weekend enthusiast who manages most of the blue square runs with aplomb, or a Downhill racer who holds his or her own in the toughest professional competition. It works because it quiets the conscious mind and engages your unconscious resources.

An active, conscious mind is like a mogul or an icy spot; it interferes with good skiing because you are *thinking* too much about body mechanics while making your way down the hill. My techniques get you to do all your thinking about the work of your body, skis, and poles during practice sessions so your conscious mind stays out of the way.

After years of thinking about the unity of mind and body, I became dissatisfied with the methods of coaching that stressed conscious thought. The methods are okay up to a point, but they don't fully correspond to what superb athletes really do in their minds to control their behavior.

To eliminate my dissatisfaction I studied psychology and counseling. Even that didn't help. So I decided to go to the sources—the athletes themselves, in this case intermediate, expert, and world-class skiers. I asked them how they used their minds and emotions to develop and control their skiing skills. My training as a Master Practitioner in Neuro-Linguistic Programming (NLP) provided me with the knowledge to ask the right questions and the skills to uncover the skiers' conscious and unconscious mental processes. (See page 14 for a description of NLP.)

As I talked informally with people, I became convinced that the management of fear could be the central theme of a useful book for skiers. I spent hundreds of hours interviewing top skiers about their fears on the slopes. I discovered how and what they were thinking, consciously and unconsciously, as they broke through the barriers of their fears.

I questioned skiers about how they mentally regained balance when they lost control during a run. I found out how they mentally prepared for meeting reasonable challenges of new and difficult trails. I asked them how they restored their confidence to ski again after serious injuries. And I probed their brains to find out what the internal mental experience of fear was like. Much of the book is the result of this exploration.

From what these and other athletes have told me, along with what I'd learned from psychology and my coaching experience, I created a model of human behavior and counseling. I coined a word that describes my perspective of how the mind works in sports: *metaskills.* It refers to the interaction between emotions and thoughts that produces skillful athletic performance, most of which are outside conscious awareness.

To refine my metaskills techniques I initially worked for two years with eighty elite athletes (male and female, ages eight to thirty-five) in eleven sports. The model that evolved has been working successfully for about twelve years with all kinds of athletes. This book contains descriptions of the techniques that are most appropriate for skiers.

I describe in Part I the fundamentals of the mind's role

in skiing: how your mind operates, how to deepen awareness of your unique mental processes, and how you can improve each run by capitalizing on your past experiences and inner emotional resources.

Part II contains descriptions of specific techniques, about thirty-five in all, that can be applied to your method of thinking and the unique way you respond emotionally to weather conditions and the nature of the terrain. These techniques are designed to help you achieve better concentration, heightened motivation, consistency of performance, increased self-confidence, improved skills, and more enjoyment.

Also in Part II, I describe how you can mentally plan your run down a challenging hill, how you can run your brain to regain control when conditions get rough, and how you can mentally prepare yourself to extend your ability and meet new challenges on the mountain. I also present some techniques that focus on controlling pain and faster healing after injury.

The psychological perspective that I emphasize is one of understanding *how* skiers mentally control their performance. I'm not interested in uncovering the deep-seated, psychoanalytic reasons *why* they don't ski well; nor am I interested in the mechanical errors in poor performance. These approaches tap and reinforce negative ideas that perpetuate bad skiing.

Believe it or not, you already possess all the necessary internal resources for skiing well. Your beliefs and values, your emotions, and your thought processes all unconsciously regulate the quality of your skiing. The trick is to uncover them and put them to work.

What makes this book different from other skiing books is that I help you pay attention to *how* you think—how you run your brain. Using metaskills techniques, you will learn how to run your brain differently by practicing thought processes while skiing on easy slopes or even sitting in an armchair.

The mind games in this book are designed to turn your skiing mind from conscious control to automatic pilot. Except for brief, conscious mental planning of the route or line for each section of a trail, the ultimate goal is to have your unconscious mind in complete control. Seldom will you consciously need to apply any metaskills techniques while actually skiing. If you've learned them well, they'll "kick in" automatically, just as your best carving of the snow automatically follows a grooved pattern. Ultimately you'll be able to ski without any conscious thought, the way you shake hands or tie your shoes.

Metaskills techniques will improve your skiing because they focus on learning about and using the unique workings of your mind. Specifically, you'll learn how to: expand and modify your sensory acuity so that your thinking is changed; identify the internal resources needed to ski well; control your emotions with thought; allow your automatic, mental skiing programs to take control; and put your conscious mind on hold, out of the way.

All of these mental abilities will increase the number of choices you will have to control your skiing. Of course, if you're a novice, they won't allow you to ski black-diamond trails immediately. Still, they will help you to make better turns, if that's a goal, or gradually to manage steeper pitches or moguls with confidence. Furthermore, the effects of all of your newly acquired mental skills will ripple outward to make other parts of your life more satisfying.

How to Use This Book

Use this book to supplement the work of your skiing instructor, whose job is to teach you the actual mechanics of skiing. Read it whenever you have a spare moment and refer to it during your practice sessions.

The time frame for learning any one of the techniques can range from half an hour to a few weeks. It all depends on what you want and how much energy you apply to achieve it. Mental practice, like physical practice, also requires time.

I can't emphasize often enough that the best way to learn my techniques is to experience them firsthand, while *doing* something—poling out of the starting gate, for instance, or carving parallel turns in powder—something very precise *on the hill* that you would like to improve. Find out what happens to the way you ski after applying a technique; then analyze and evaluate its usefulness in terms of your improvement.

This book can be used as a workbook, a learning companion when you're practicing the skills taught by your skiing instructor. For a while, don't leave home for the slopes without it. Treat it as a learning manual to help you use your mind and emotions to get what you want. Read Part I carefully and do the exercises presented there. This will make the rest of the book more meaningful. After doing the Sherlock Holmes Exercise and learning how to "anchor" your internal resources, read Part II casually. Then study and use the appropriate techniques when something in your performance needs to be fine-tuned or some aspect of your temperament needs to be controlled.

Keep in mind that some techniques are more appropriate than others for you. The final chapter, "*Après* Ski," tells you how to identify your desired outcomes and guides you in selecting different metaskills techniques to achieve them. However, I encourage you to pay attention only to the crucial mechanics you want to improve. I'm a firm believer in the notion "If it ain't broke, don't fix it."

Setting aside mental practice time is essential to learning my techniques. Merely *reading* this book is *not enough*. And *use only one technique at a time.* Learn how it works and determine whether it fits your mental style. Some of my best clients initially experienced "brainlock" when they tried to use too many of my exercises at once. They learned—the hard way—the importance of exploring one of them at a time.

Now go to the next page and start looking for the mind games that will be most useful for you. Happy exploring.

The
Fundamentals

Learning how your mind works, how to make it work more efficiently, and how to tap your internal resources are the first steps to master in the skier's mind game. The initial part of this book is as fundamental as learning how to adjust the bindings of your skis. Not until the fundamentals are learned will you be able to use your mind so that you accomplish what may seem self-contradictory: carving turns with effortless effort and mindless concentration.

Settle back into an easy chair now and put aside your point of view about skiing. In this first part of the book I'll present some basic ideas about the mind and how to run your brain. Then I'll ask you to become your own investigator in exploring how your mind actually guides you down the hill safely, balanced, and in control. After explaining how expert skiers run their brains while skiing, I'll provide you with special exercises to expand and refine your mental capacities. Finally, you'll learn a special way to uncover and use your internal mental and emotional resources to meet the challenges of skiing.

ONE

On the Way Up

Amy Hill was one of only six members of the 1984 Best Ever Program for young Canadian skiers who trained with the Canadian National Ski Team and aspired to be a member of the '88 Olympic team. She had a problem as common—and frustrating—as a cold. A barrier of fear was preventing her from executing certain difficult turns well. After completing one turn and preparing to attack the next, she would pull back from moving up and forward on her skis. Instead of rolling from one edge and releasing to the flat of her skis, she went directly from edge to edge without releasing and failed to extend her body upward. The result: loss of speed or a fall.

Amy asked me the usual question posed by athletes when performance goes sour: "What's wrong? Why can't I do what I'm supposed to do?" Answering these questions isn't very useful because it reinforces mistakes. So I focused on the solution instead of on the problem.

Since Amy already knew how to attack turns from her

extensive Downhill competitive experience, I had her re-create, in her mind, a beautifully executed turn on a transition from a flat section over a knoll into a pitch. For example: Was the day sunny? How did the turn look and feel? Did she hear the sound of her edges? Then I put her through a series of exercises, on and off the snow, designed to train her unconscious mind to perform that beautifully executed turn automatically whenever she wanted to.

Amy knew how to make good turns at transitions. I merely helped her realize that—and never to misplace that ability. I find that once a skill is locked in the mind, it can be retrieved, appropriately enough, with a key. Amy found the key rather quickly, and now uses it whenever she wants to ski confidently.

Amy's key is a metaphor, the unusual thought of a "puffed pink balloon." It's a metaphor that integrates her mind, body, and emotions, and allows her unconscious mind to let her skis run and turn aggressively. How Amy created that metaphor will be fully explained in a subsequent chapter. For now, it's only important to realize that all the mind games in this book reflect Amy's experience. They are unusual and fun; and they work.

Mind-Body Unity

The fundamental principle underlying my perspective of human behavior in general, and athletic performance in particular, is that mind, body, and emotions are inextricably interwoven. It's sort of like having your two boots pressed together as one as you parallel ski.

Thought influences feelings and performance; feelings

affect thought and performance; and performance affects thought and feelings. Specifically the quality and consistency of your athletic performance depend upon *how* you think and *how* you feel emotionally.

The metaskills techniques presented in this book were designed to affect your thought processes and emotional states, with only minimal attention to the content of your thoughts.

The Unconscious Mind in Sports

Think about thinking. Thinking while executing sports skills is detrimental to superb performance because it destroys intense concentration. In Zen meditation the ideal state of concentration is paying attention to nothing. This applies to skiing as well, but it is extremely difficult to achieve. The next best way of thinking is to pay attention to *only one thing.* It might be watching the tips of your skis with peripheral vision, feeling your feet press and turn your skis, hearing a phrase spoken in your head, or seeing a metaphorical image in your mind's eye—whatever works for you.

For instance, if Mary Lou Retton had had to process mentally every bit of information necessary to execute that perfect 10 vault in the 1984 Olympics—feet together at takeoff, hands exactly so to get into the twist, knees bent at the precise moment while in the air—she never would have landed on a Wheaties box.

Instead, Mary Lou tied every bit of complex movement into a single word. That word was *stick.* She knew unconsciously what was necessary to achieve perfection, to "stick" a 10, and to "stick" to the mat after a flawless dismount. She used that word to trigger her unconscious mind, which automatically guided her body to achieve Olympian power and grace.

I know the paramount role the unconscious mind has in affecting human behavior. Superb athletic performance is achieved with little or no *conscious* thought given to goals, tactics, and mechanics. The clichés that reinforce this are numerous: "paralysis by analysis," "playing in the zone," and "It's like I wasn't there."

Conscious processing is entirely too slow and results in confusion. Skiing is too fast for the conscious mind. You don't think about planting your pole at the slalom gate; you just do it. While conscious attention to performance is most important during learning and practice, it is the mindless (unconscious) processes that allow for exquisite execution of skills already mastered. The more refined the athlete's performance, the more the unconscious mind is in control.

Neuro-Linguistic Programming

During the past fifteen years a new psychotechnology has emerged. It's called Neuro-Linguistic Programming (NLP); it was created by Richard Bandler and John Grinder, Ph.D. Bandler, a mathematician, and Grinder, a linguist, teamed up while studying the verbal and non-verbal communication nuances of three renowned psychotherapists: Fritz Perls, Virginia Satir, and Milton H. Erickson, M.D. Perls was a famous Gestalt therapist, initially trained by Sigmund Freud; Satir was an illustrious family therapist; and Erickson was a medical hypnotherapist who revolutionized the practice of medical hypnosis.

Bandler and Grinder observed these people at work, studied their videotapes, learned to mimic their voices and bodily mannerisms, and conversed with them about their therapeutic interventions. After several years of study, they identified, labeled, dissected, and integrated the communication patterns of the three clinicians into a codified system of concepts and techniques that they called NLP.

Essentially, NLP is used to identify how people actually regulate their behavior with their minds. Used to help people change their behavior rather quickly by changing mental processes, NLP is a vital part of my work because it emphasizes the role of the unconscious mind in regulating behavior.

In my opinion NLP is one of the most powerful psychological tools available to help people change their behavior. It is state-of-the-art theory and practice based on verbal and nonverbal communication processes. Increasing numbers of psychologists and psychiatrists are coming to recognize its usefulness in quickly overcoming phobias, compulsions, stage fright, and other debilitating behaviors. If you're interested in learning more about NLP, you'll find selected readings listed in the back of the book.

The elements of the NLP model that apply to skiing are *information processing, mental strategies, emotional states,* and *beliefs and values.*

Information Processing and Mental Strategies

Let's look a little closer at the way your skiing mind works. How does a skier know how and when to turn on the snow? For that matter, how does anyone know how to drive a car or tie his shoes? By reproducing in his mind the sights, sounds, feelings, smells, and tastes associated with how he did it in the past.

In a span of a second or two, the time it takes to pass a slalom gate, we unconsciously process as many as a hundred bits of patterned, or programmed, sensory information—sights, sounds, and feelings—to control our behavior. This programmed information, or strategy, fires off just nanoseconds in advance of a behavior such as doing a royal christie. If the skier's turning program is wrong or is interrupted, he may fall.

The mental programming we've developed for ourselves over a lifetime is much more sophisticated than anything that could be put on a floppy disk. The nice thing about our programs is that they're flexible and overlap. We can change them at a moment's notice when we sense, consciously or unconsciously, that they ought to be altered for our own best interests.

We often find several separate strategies in operation at the same time to regulate a number of different behaviors. For example, consider a skier about to ski a new trail.

First he must initiate his *decision-making* strategy to determine if the trail is within his skiing ability. If he decides to go down, his *motivation* strategy is energized to carry out that decision. Since the trail and the snow conditions are not exactly like trails he has skied before, he sets his *creativity* strategy in motion to put together a combination of turns to get him safely down the hill. Knowing exactly how to turn at each point requires that his *memory* strategy be set off.

Then, to ski the planned line, he activates a series of *performance* strategies. However, if he loses his balance or misses a turn, all of the above strategies are reactivated unconsciously, with all of them overlapping. Within several seconds, or much less time than it took you to read this, the skier triggered five separate strategies: *decision-making, motivation, creativity, memory,* and *performance.* Each strategy was somewhat dependent on the others. His unconscious thought, that which is outside awareness, was much more significant to his skiing performance than his conscious thought. And the more streamlined the mental process, the faster his reaction—or that of any athlete.

This complex form of mentally regulating human behavior is called a *cybernetic system.* Feedforward and feedback mechanisms, usually outside of conscious awareness, are constantly in operation as the athlete performs. The internal regulatory systems of the body are constantly comparing ongoing internal and external sensory data with the output of the muscles that bring about our intended behavior, such as rapidly making a number of short-radius turns close to the fall line of a steep slope.

Let's say you're approaching a mogul. To plan your turn at the mogul, you need both present and past information to feed forward into the actual turning process. Some of the important, present information consists of the speed with which you're approaching the mogul, the angle of approach, the nature of the snow, the shape of the terrain in front of and beyond the mogul, the feel of your balance and control, and the feel of your edges on the snow. This present information, most of which is processed unconsciously, partly regulates your turn.

Past, remembered information is also fed forward into the turning process. This includes rapid memories—in the form of images, sounds, and feelings—related to how you successfully turned at similar moguls before: the angle of attack, the speed, the action of your poles, and other similar mechanics. This information is largely processed unconsciously, too.

Comparisons of these two kinds of ongoing information, past and present, are continuously and rapidly being made in your brain automatically and unconsciously. If the feedback information doesn't match the feedforward information, more information about the present and the immediate future must be accessed to help you change the way you move. If you have to turn before you get matching information, a spill is likely.

When the comparisons between feedforward and feedback information match, however, no change in the planned turn is initiated. *Voilà!* You make a smoothly executed turn at the mogul, feeling like Alberto Tomba or Diann Roffe. Your unconscious mind is so sensitive it even reacts and adjusts to an unexpected patch of ice.

Metaskills techniques are designed to affect the basic elements of the skier's unconscious mental strategies. They are based on how the brain actually works when the conscious mind doesn't interfere with it. The techniques are designed to change or stabilize a skier's performance by changing how, in his mind, he processes sights, sounds, feelings, smells, and tastes.

Just-Right Emotional State

Although each person's programmed mental strategies for skiing are different, common to all of us is the fact that we must be in an appropriate mood or emotional state for a particular strategy to be activated. And each of us has unique just-right states for accomplishing different tasks. Let's say you're starting down a steep pitch. In the just-right state, all the auditory, visual, and kinesthetic information of having done that task before is automatically and unconsciously fired off before and during the run. However, if you're not in the right state, the strategy will be defective because key elements of it are missing.

I'm sure you know that the state you want to be in while skiing on powder on a moderately sloped, back-bowl trail will be much different from the state you want to be in when you are attacking the mountain during a slalom race. For the former you want a smooth-flowing effort; for the latter you want an aggressive feeling of your edges as you muster the power and control to hug the fall line.

Because your emotional state determines whether you will ski well, many of my metaskills techniques are based on identifying and anchoring the appropriate internal states for skiing different kinds of trails. When they're properly anchored, the appropriate strategies will be engaged to regulate automatically how you ski different pitches, flats, knolls, and transitions. How to get into those just-right states is described later.

Beliefs and Values

Skiers can't leave their beliefs and values behind when they head out to the mountain. A belief is something accepted as true without certainty of proof; a value is a standard or criterion by which you determine if something is important to you. Both serve as guides in making decisions, and both are at work during every skiing run, affecting the skier's moods from moment to moment. Since moods influence mental strategies, beliefs and values either facilitate or intrude on what could be a very pleasurable day of skiing.

Compare the emotional responses of three different skiers on approaching an intermediate trail. One skier, the macho type, views the run as a way to impress his girlfriend. Overly confident, he poles over the edge, hooting and hollering as he skis recklessly down the hill, frightening even the most confident skiers as he passes much too close to them.

A second skier, the macho man's girlfriend, accurately views the trail as entirely too steep for her ability. Nonetheless, she had acquiesced to her boyfriend's insistence that she could ski the trail. Against her better judgment she joined him on the lift to the top. There she is—trembling. Rather than chicken out, she snowplows her way to the bottom, feeling embarrassed, and resolves to ski trails suited to her ability.

The third skier is well aware of his competence and believes he can manage the trail if he prepares himself mentally for the task. After planning his route to the bottom, he skis each section, stopping when necessary if he loses balance and control.

Each of the skiers brings to the mountain a belief about himself that affects how he responds emotionally to the trail. Each reflects a set of values as they make their way to the bottom. One values getting attention, ignoring the safety of others; another mistakenly values pleasing her boyfriend in spite of her own fears. The third believes in skiing up to his ability, valuing his own safety. In many instances, changing your beliefs and reordering your values can affect your skiing performance and the degree to which you enjoy your day on the mountain. Certain meta-skills techniques focus on these concerns.

Communication and Change

The techniques in this book are forms of communication that are intended to change your behavior. They are designed to influence your mental strategies, your emotional states, and your beliefs and values. My instructions are deliberately intended to affect the *way* you perceive the environment and the *way* you communicate with yourself —the *way* you run your brain. Your attention will be limited to how you process relevant sights, sounds, and feelings. It will not be focused on how to manipulate your skis and poles. My techniques do not teach you the physical mechanics of the stem christie, a snowplow, hockey stops, and other maneuvers. That's the skiing instructor's job. However, while you are learning the mechanics of skiing, or after you have learned them, my mental techniques will help you execute them better.

Self-Hypnosis

Some of my exercises are based on hypnosis, although highly sophisticated daydreaming might be as good a way to describe some of what actually happens. It's Walter Mitty stuff, nothing scary. Most athletes, in fact, are in a trance, a profound altered state, when they perform superbly.

Admit it, now. You've transported yourself, perhaps at a traffic light or at the office, to the slopes of Aspen, Taos, Killington, or St. Moritz, where you ski with abandon in the crisp, sunny quiet of nature. In your mind you weave among trees, jump ledges, and carve turns in powder, finishing off the day with supper before a crackling fire in the lodge. Or mentally you've seen yourself at Val d'Isère needing to clear only one more section to win the Downhill gold, not to mention the glory and fistfuls of dollars. Mentally you see and feel an array of your best turns and jumps.

Growing up, you watched Arnold Palmer, Billie Jean King, Jean-Claude Killy, and other wondrous athletes. Later you tried to mimic their seemingly unique motions in your mind—and then scooted out to work on duplicating them. What surely never entered your mind at the time is that you were using a kind of self-hypnosis. I have techniques that use that concept, one of which can help you ski like a World Cup pro.

Let's get started.

T W O

The Sherlock Holmes Exercise: Discover How Your Mind Regulates Your Skiing

This is a must-read chapter; it's fundamental to everything that follows. Practically all of my techniques deal with "going inside" and retrieving past experiences. These remembered experiences are resources to be used to build your confidence and make your skiing more balanced and controlled. And being able to identify these resources on command is essential to applying my unique mind games. How to go about doing that is what you'll learn in this chapter.

Be Sherlock Holmes for a while and discover the important elements of how you run your brain while skiing. All you have to think about is being wonderful—in your own mind, at least. As Sherlock you'll be searching for clues to what makes your skiing so special. These clues will be in the form of sights, sounds, and feelings, some of which will eventually become important cues to running your brain effectively while on the hill.

It's important that you go to a quiet place to do this exercise. When you do, you will recall when you made an exceptionally good run down a challenging trail. You'll think about a very specific turn, traverse, jump, or stop, not an entire run or even a section of a course. Out of the hundreds or thousands of maneuvers you've made, simply select one that made you proud. Perhaps it was a short-radius turn on the fall line; or maybe you rode a really clean edge as you carved a wide turn. Perhaps you can recall a time when you regained your balance skillfully after a scary slide on ice. Just remember one specific skill that you performed well.

The idea of this exercise is to uncover some of the crucial elements of the mental program that regulates your movement on the hill; these elements comprise what is known as a strategy. That strategy contains a programmed series of representations of sensory bits of information—sights, sounds, and feelings. I use the letters V, A, and K to signify those sensory bits; V is for visual, A is for auditory, and K is for kinesthetic—muscle and joint feelings, feelings on the surface of your body, and the bodily sensations associated with emotions.

During the execution of a skiing maneuver—starting with getting your body and skis into the proper position, continuing with adjusting your balance, and ending with the completion of a turn, or a stop—your mind processes as many as a hundred or more bits of sensory information with machine-gun rapidity. Just a few of those sensory representations are in your conscious awareness. The rest are processed unconsciously because of the speed with which you are moving on the snow and the quickness of the maneuver itself.

Sensory information consists of specific internal sights, sounds, and feelings representing specific *past* experiences of preparing for and executing a skiing maneuver; it also consists of *ongoing* internal and external sights, sounds, and feelings that are occurring as you ski.

Your Task as Sherlock Holmes

The way you watch your past performance, the way you listen to the sounds associated with it, and the kind of bodily sensations that you pay attention to will determine your success as Sherlock Holmes. The more thorough you are, the more you'll discover the clues that make your performance so good.

The main questions to ask yourself as you relive that maneuver are these: What were the things you saw, the things you heard, and the things you felt that let you know where to position yourself and when and how to move your body, skis, and poles on the hill? What did you see, hear, and feel that let you know that your movements were either okay or needed to be corrected?

You're looking for clues—in the form of certain A's, V's, and K's—that control what you already know how to do but may not know that you know. You might notice, for example, that your hands had a firm but light grip on the poles; that K is a clue. Or you may hear the sound of the skis on the snow as you ride an edge; that A is a clue. Or you might notice the reflections of light on the snow as you approach a turn; that V is a clue. Make mental notes of the A's, V's, and K's as you go along. At the end of the search you can write down what you discovered.

Later you will learn which of these clues are of significance to the way you mentally regulate your skiing. Some of them will be of no consequence; others will be vital and will serve as visual, auditory, and kinesthetic cues to stimulate your unconscious mental processes. The metaskills exercises in Part II will help you know which sensory bits of information are the most useful.

Now let's begin.

Step 1. General Review

In your mind, go back to the time and place when you made that fine maneuver. First, just do a general, overall mental review of it, as if you're watching a movie. Forget about the spectators if there were any. Just pay attention to the sensory bits of information—what you saw, heard, and felt—that regulated your skiing maneuver. Those bits of information could be related to how you approached the particular point on the trail, your body position, your grip on the poles, the pressure of your feet on the skis, and the mood or state you were in while you were executing that maneuver.

See the slope of the trail; observe the shadows and reflection of light on the snow; notice the position of your hands and the direction of your skis. Notice the light and shadows and the brightness of the colors. See the images that were in your mind as you were making that maneuver. Maybe you were imagining yourself passing closely to a gate or tree. Notice the location of the imaginary screen on which you were projecting those internal images; see if the screen is tilted.

Hear again what you heard then, both outside and inside your mind. Perhaps you heard the rhythmic schuss of your skis; maybe you heard music in your head or your own voice giving yourself silent instructions. Pay attention to the loudness, pitch, and tempo of the sounds. Also notice the location of the sounds you're hearing in your mind and the direction in which they are traveling—forward, sideways, up, down.

As you see and hear those things, *feel* again what you felt as you executed that maneuver—the coordinated movements of your body and the tension and relaxation of your muscles. Also, become aware of the mood or emotional state you were in as you skied.

Now it's time to get out Holmes's magnifying glass and ear trumpet and pay more attention to the details of what you saw, heard, and felt back then, on the outside and inside your mind.

Step 2. Identifying the V's—the Sights

First pay attention to what you saw on the outside, as if you were right there on the hill making that maneuver—the trail in front of you, the tips of your skis, your hands gripping the poles. I call these images "regular" pictures. Then shift your way of watching so that you see yourself skiing as if looking through someone else's eyes, like watching yourself skiing on videotape. It might be helpful to imagine stepping out of your body, walking a few paces, and then turning to gaze on a piece of athletic magic about to unfold from your favorite athletic star—you.

From this visual perspective as a spectator, called the meta position, take the role of Sherlock Holmes and search for something you didn't know you knew that made your maneuver so good. (If you have difficulty making meta pictures, turn to page 198 in Appendix A.)

As you watch yourself perform, change the image of yourself—the *meta picture*—to color if it's black and white; change it to black and white if it's in color. If the picture is bright, make it dull; if dull, make it bright. If the picture is sharply defined, make it fuzzy; if fuzzy, make it defined. Notice what happens to the quality of your performance as you vary the internal images this way; your performance may get better or worse. Does it get better or worse as you vary the color, brightness, focus, and size of the pictures? Make mental notes about the kinds of images that made your performance good.

Now make regular pictures of the maneuver, no longer watching yourself. See again what you saw while preparing for and making the maneuver. Vary the color, brightness, and definition of what you saw as you were skiing down the hill. Continue to search for the important clues that let you know when and how to move your skis. Look for the clues that let you know whether your movements were okay or needed to be changed. Notice what happens to the quality of your performance as you vary the images. Does it improve or deteriorate?

Now take a moment to become aware of the *internal* images, the ones you had in your mind *then,* when you were on the hill. What were they, if any? Did you see an image of your hands up? Did you see an imaginary line directing you to a turning point? How were these internal images helpful? Vary the color, brightness, and definition of these internal images; notice what happens to the quality of your performance as you vary them. Does it get better or worse?

Step 3. Identifying the A's—the Sounds

While watching your past performance, using either regular or meta pictures, hear again what you heard then. Listen to the sounds directly associated with moving your skis. Listen to the sounds in the surrounding environment and the sounds in your mind. For instance, on the outside you might hear your breathing, your poles striking a gate, or your edges digging into the snow. On the inside, in your mind, you might hear silence or your own voice giving yourself instructions.

If the sounds were loud, make them barely audible; if hardly heard, turn up the volume. If they were high-pitched tones, make them low; if low-pitched, make them high. If they were harmonious, make them discordant and unpleasant; if unpleasant, make them harmonious. If the tempo of the sounds was an even beat, make it irregular; if irregular, make it even. And while you're varying the sounds, notice whether the quality of your performance improves or deteriorates. Continue, as Sherlock Holmes, to listen for the important sounds that were present when your movements were just as they were supposed to be. Are some sounds more important than others? Make a mental note of your discoveries.

Step 4. Identifying the K's—the Bodily Sensations

As you relive the maneuver over and over, pay close attention to (1) the feelings of your coordinated movements, (2) the feelings of certain parts of your body that were essential to making the maneuver, (3) the amount of energy and tension you felt in various muscles, and (4) the emotional feelings or mood you were in *while* you were skiing.

You might feel a number of things as you do this exercise. For instance, you might feel the turn of your shoulders facing down the hill, or the flexing of your knees, or the shifting of your weight from one ski to the other.

Now, in your mind, vary the way you moved. If your movements were quick, slow them down; if slow, speed them up. If you were exerting a lot of energy and pressure, relax the effort; if effortless, increase the tension of your muscles. While varying those feelings, notice what happens to the quality of your performance. Does it get better or worse? As Sherlock Holmes, continue to identify and make mental notes of the feelings that made your performance so good.

The emotional feelings you had in your body *while,* not after, you were executing a maneuver are as important as the muscular feelings associated with making the maneuver. Those emotional sensations represent the mood or state you were in. Feel them again. Perhaps they were feelings of lightness, tingling, warmth, tension, or pulsing that were present in parts of your body. Vary the intensity of these emotional feelings and find out what happens to the quality of the maneuver. Does it get better or worse when you increase or decrease the intensity? What amount of intensity is just right for making it the best possible maneuver?

Step 5. Putting It All Together

After you've gone through seeing, listening, and feeling, have some fun with reliving that past performance. Pretend you've got a videotape of it and watch it while using the variable-speed and direction buttons on the video control.

First run the tape twice as fast as normal, then four times as fast, and then bring the speed back to normal. In addition, slow the tape to half speed and then to one frame at a time. Be sure to bring the tape back up to normal speed. With each variation in speed, carefully pay attention, as before, to discovering new visual, auditory, and kinesthetic clues that seem to be essential to skiing so well.

Now run the tape in reverse—in normal, slow, and fast motion—again paying attention to new sights, sounds, and feelings. Finish by running the tape forward again. Keep in mind that the usefulness of the sensory information you uncover as Sherlock will be determined as you work with the metaskills techniques described later on.

Here is a summary of the steps to follow:

SHERLOCK HOLMES EXERCISE

1. Go to a quiet room. After a while you'll be able to do it—during practice—out on the hill.

2. Remember a specific maneuver that you performed exceptionally well during a run.

3. See everything you can see about the maneuver; hear everything you can hear about the maneuver; feel everything you can feel about the maneuver.

4. Vary what you see (from color to black and white, from fuzzy to clear); change the sounds (from loud to soft, from pleasant to unpleasant); alter your feelings (from quick to slow, from relaxed to tense).

5. Remember the details. Write the important ones down if it'll help. You'll be using them later.

Reactions to the
Sherlock Holmes Exercise

Although there is some typical sensory information that most skiers pay attention to while they're performing a maneuver, each person has his or her unique way of processing and giving meaning to particular A's, V's, and K's. There are no right or wrong sensory cues for skiing. It's what you do with them that's important.

To help you understand how expert skiers process information, I'll share with you some of what I learned from them when they used the Sherlock Holmes Exercise. Their mental processes are often unusual and quite sophisticated. I'll identify both their *internal* and *external* sensory representations.

Internal sensations—what a person sees, hears, and feels inside, in the mind—are classified in NLP lingo as "downtime." External sensations—what a person sees, hears, and feels that come directly from the environment or are directly associated with movements that control their skiing maneuvers—are classified in NLP lingo as "uptime."

What the Expert Skiers See—the
Internal (Downtime) V's

All expert skiers I've talked to imagine the actual path they want to follow before they start down the hill. The paths they imagine include the locations where they want to turn. Many skiers also visualize making each turn just before they get to it. Chapter Four contains detailed explanations of how mentally to plan and rehearse a particular run.

What the Expert Skiers See—the External (Uptime) V's

Uptime *visual* cues that expert skiers attend to are familiar, I'm sure, because most skiers are sensitive to them. They include: the angle of the pitch and width of the trail; reflections of light and shadows on the snow; icy patches, rocks, bumps, knolls, moguls, trees, and lift towers; other skiers; slalom gates; and "billy bags."

What the Expert Skiers Hear—the Internal (Downtime) A's

The internal auditory information processed by expert skiers almost always consists of short, positive statements or commands. Ben-Henry Jones, a senior skier, praises himself regularly when he skis well. He silently asserts, "Good! Good!" Jerry Beilinson, an expert skier, frequently reminds himself when he approaches difficult turns on very steep terrain, "Be aggressive! Attack! Go for it!" In a different vein, Chris Parrot, a former U.S. Junior Olympic competitor in all the alpine events, sings a 1965 Beatles tune, "If I Fell in Love with You," in his head; the rhythm of the tune matches the rhythm of his turns.

Many other expert skiers, however, are aware only of internal silence when they are skiing well; they listen primarily to the external, rhythmic schuss of their skis. When skiing poorly, they silently admonish themselves for their mistakes. One senior PSIA instructor says to himself, "I hope no one sees me" when he goofs. Matt King, an expert skier, shouts in his mind, "BRAKES!" when he gets out of control.

When they perform poorly, most skiers give themselves verbal instructions that actually interfere with their performance; the speed of their words is too slow and cannot keep up with the speed of the run. Consequently they lose their concentration.

What the Expert Skiers Hear—the External (Uptime) A's

The significant uptime *auditory* cues that expert skiers listen to are: the rhythmic sound of their skis as they turn; the different pitch of the sound of the edges—varying from a soft, quiet schuss to a loud, scratchy "gritch"; and the clatter of their skis on the hard snow.

What the Expert Skiers Feel—the Internal (Downtime) K's

The way skiers feel emotionally is absolutely crucial to balanced and controlled skiing. As you might expect, the emotional state most conducive for good skiing varies from person to person and from time to time.

When skiing beautifully on an Aspen Downhill course, Amy Hill felt as if she was "part of the air"; this was manifested in her bodily sensations as lightness and hollowness, as if the wind could pass through her body. When she won the World Cup Super G in Japan in 1988, Liisa Savijarvi, a former member of the Canadian National Ski Team, said, "I skied like I was unconscious. . . . It was so much fun!" Jerry Beilinson said, "I had a feeling of calm in my gut" when he first successfully skied the Paradise Headwall at Crested Butte in Colorado.

As previously indicated, skiers need to be in a just-right state to ski well, and this state changes for each skiing maneuver. The ability to generate various just-right states is undoubtedly the most important skill you can learn.

These states are manifested by internal emotional K's and will vary from person to person. During her victory run for the gold at the 1976 Innsbruck Olympics, Kathy Kreiner had a feeling of "effortless flow." The way she generated this just-right state was to do some free skiing for about an hour and a half just before her race. Chapters Five and Six are devoted to exercises designed to generate just-right states quickly.

What Expert Skiers Feel—the External (Uptime) K's

The most important uptime *kinesthetic* cues of expert skiers are associated with: knee flexion, leg strength, shoulder turn and hip rotation; comfortable grip on the poles; pressure of the soles of the feet on the skis, pressure of the edges, and the "bite" of the skis at the beginning of a turn; the slipperiness of the skis; and weight shifts and balance.

For example, Dave Hill is acutely aware of the pressure of his legs against his boots. When he feels the boot on the back of his legs he knows he is leaning back into the hill, a no-no! When Kathy Kreiner is turning properly she feels increased pressure of her boot against her shin. Liisa Savijarvi knows she is attacking the hill when she feels her hands "up and forward."

Some Important
Questions and Answers

The Sherlock Holmes Exercise might inspire the following:

Q: What am I supposed to see, hear, and feel?

A: Whatever you *do* see, hear, and feel. Each one of us has developed our own set of sensory cues that regulate our behavior; some are more sensitive than others. Also, some people become so involved as Sherlock that they think they're actually on the hill; others simply remain aware of what's around them in the room. So don't go into this exercise with preconceived ideas.

Q: How come you had me change what I saw, heard, and felt so often? Why change colors to black and white and then back? Why change the tension in my muscles? Why change the volume of the sound?

A: Technically, I'm dealing with what we call *sensory submodalities* (see Appendix A). Modalities are seeing, hearing, and feeling. The other modalities of smelling and tasting exist, but they are of little consequence for our purposes. Submodalities are the refined elements of seeing, hearing, and feeling such as color, volume, and tension. When you vary the submodalities of sight, sound, and feeling, learning —and change—are most likely to occur.

Q: Since I can't see and hear very much going on in my mind, how can I be a good Sherlock?

A: Although it's possible for most people to be 100 percent tuned into their inner sounds and have exquisite imagery, some just haven't paid much attention to these sensory happenings, just as some people aren't as sensitive to their bodily sensations as others are.

However, if after doing the Sherlock Holmes Exercise you still have difficulty making pictures in your mind, recalling internal sounds, or feeling a variety of physical sensations, you can use the questions and exercises in Appendix A to expand and refine the quality of your built-in sensory awareness. The better it is, the easier it will be for you to apply metaskills techniques.

Q: How do I determine the significance of all the internal and external A's, V's, and K's? There were so many that I don't know how to evaluate them.

A: Just make notes of the sights, sounds, and feelings that *seem* to be important. Postpone analyzing them. When you come to learning the various metaskills techniques later, you can then decide which are the most useful.

Now that you know how to retrieve the details of past experience—the uptime and downtime A's, V's, and K's— let's start playing some of my mind games so that your skiing gets better.

THREE

Anchoring: Tapping Your Inner Resources

This chapter is your guide to making the most of your past experience. You will learn how to identify the kinds of internal resources you have within to ski better, and how to make them automatically available for application on the hill.

Mental Aspects of Skiing

The mental aspects of skiing consist of four main tasks. One task consists of mapping the route to the bottom of the hill. This mapping function occurs at the start of each run and at the beginning of each section of the trail on the way down. The second mental task consists of generating sufficient confidence and courage to ski each section of each trail before you start or continue down the hill. The third task involves getting yourself in the just-right state to accomplish specific skiing maneuvers, such as different kinds of turns, traverses, jumps, and stops. The fourth task involves intense concentration on the conditions of the trail —characteristics of the snow, contour of the terrain, location of bumps and obstacles, and potential turning points.

Since the speed of descent is frequently much too fast for any kind of conscious thought about how to control your body and your emotional state, the skier's mind must be primed consciously *before* each run so the unconscious mind is free to operate *during* the run. This done, your unconscious mind can automatically generate the appropriate just-right state and automatically control your skiing maneuvers. All of these automatic processes occur naturally unless you allow your conscious mind to disrupt them.

In other words, *before* you start down the hill, your route to the bottom must be planned, efficient mental strategies must have already been developed, and the just-right emotional states must be ready to emerge when needed. If you don't preplan, conscious thought about where and how to ski *during* the run will interfere with automatic unconscious functioning and can result in a loss of balance and control, a fall, and possible injury.

Basic to preplanning is knowing how to access and anchor (hold stable) the mental resources needed for safe and enjoyable skiing. After you have learned this anchoring process, we'll turn our attention in later chapters to the specifics of mapping the route, generating confidence and courage, accessing specific internal resources, and maintaining concentration.

Your Internal Resources

You have all sorts of resources stored in your memory bank that can be used to generate appropriate states of mind for skiing well. The extent of your memory is unbelievable. "It's in there"—all the sensory information associated with all your experiences—as the ad for the ingredients of Prego spaghetti sauce claims. The trick is to get it out.

Some of the resource states useful for skiing include optimism, eagerness, determination, confidence, calmness, inventiveness, hopefulness, acceptance, and patience. Optimism helps you think positively about your skiing ability; eagerness and determination serve to motivate you to refine your abilities; confidence allows you to approach danger with alertness and without undue fear; calmness can help restore balance after losing control on a difficult part of the trail; inventiveness and hopefulness are needed to create new tactics to avoid injury; acceptance prevents frustration and anger from taking over when you make mistakes; and patience permits you to accept skiing less difficult trails until you have developed sufficient expertise to manage the black diamonds.

Other useful resources include past experiences related to learning all sorts of physical skills. In these experiences are the basic resources for skiing well, such as balance, power, strength, energy, rhythm, coordination, and control. Your past experiences also contain unconscious mental strategies for managing steep pitches, making good turns and jumps on all kinds of snow surfaces, and skiing the flats as fast as the wind.

Identifying the Right Resources

By now you've probably assumed that you're about to learn to put yourself into the right frame of mind—confident, optimistic, patient—at will. But first you must decide *which* resources to call up from your past experiences. You'll know this by asking yourself these basic questions:

- Specifically, what kind of skiing maneuvers do I want to make?
- What stops me from skiing a particular course or trail well? What interferes with my plotting a safe and fast route and making turns the way I know I can?

For the first question, knowing what you want to do on the course in front of you will guide you to identify previous times when you've successfully executed similar maneuvers on the slopes, or when you had lessons and practice sessions on those maneuvers.

To facilitate accessing the appropriate memories, it's important that you know what you need to see, hear, and feel to ski the way you want to. Then as you go into your memory, as Sherlock Holmes, you can more readily access experiences that contain those same kinds of sights, sounds, and feelings. You can transfer the A's, V's, and K's from past experiences to what you want to do on the trail in front of you.

The nature of the emotional state present during past performances is perhaps the most important K to transfer to the upcoming experience. It will be that state you will want to stabilize or anchor; I'll get to this process shortly. After you've anchored that state effectively, you will be more likely to achieve your desired outcome than if no state is identified and anchored.

Frequently, skiers don't know what they want to do. So asking the second and third questions becomes appropriate. Often it's your emotional state that stops you from skiing well. As I have already stated, if you change to a just-right emotional state your normally executed programmed maneuvers will return. Consequently, by paying close attention to the mood you're in when you goof, you may have the answer to what's stopping you. Perhaps you have been feeling annoyed, impatient, skeptical, despairing, or hopeless. After identifying this stopper state, all that's necessary is to replace it with its opposite.

If it isn't your mood or state of consciousness that's interfering with your skiing well, then maybe your conscious mind is distracting your unconscious mind from carrying out its automatic tasks—that is, your internal mental strategy is out of whack. To discover if your conscious mind is the stopper, it is useful to use a metaskills technique called Discovering Difference, found on page 122, to make the necessary corrections. This technique consists of comparing what goes on in your mind when you ski well with how your mind operates when you mess up. The differences between the two reveal the factors that inhibit your performance.

Uncovering the factors that stop you from performing the way you know you can isn't always as easy as it may seem. Sometimes it might be impossible to discover all the factors that keep you from achieving your desired outcome. You may need the help of a skiing professional to refine your skiing mechanics; or you might profit from the help of a skilled sports counselor to deal with unconscious conflicts that could be interfering with maintaining the mood you need to be in to ski well.

Regardless of what factors may be disruptive, knowing

how to identify and use your internal resources is a valuable process in itself.

Accessing Internal Resources

Fortunately, NLP has formalized the normal human process of tapping past experiences and making them automatically available for use in present situations. The Sherlock Holmes Exercise is part of this process. By reliving past experiences in full detail, you'll be pleasantly surprised to discover that you have more resources for skiing better than you thought you had. When you discover this, you'll trust yourself more and build your self-confidence.

Anchoring is another part of the process that makes your internal resources—your past experiences and feelings, still stored in your subconscious—automatically available to ski better in spite of conditions that conspire to make skiing difficult. Anchors keep your resources stabilized so your skiing can become more effective and enjoyable.

Let's now turn to the process of anchoring in general. Later you'll learn how to use a variety of anchors for skiing well on different terrain and under different snow conditions.

What Is an Anchor?

You probably already know what an anchor is and how it works, but you may not know that you know. It is either an internal or an external sight, sound, feeling, smell, or taste

—a stimulus—that triggers the complex mix of sensory details associated with a particular past experience. When you see an old photograph of yourself as a child, it usually stirs up memories of that time in your life. Similarly, when you see five intertwined colored circles you might think of the Olympics. It's the same with a special song.

Our conscious and unconscious thoughts—what we see, hear, feel, smell, and taste internally—directly affect our moods or internal emotional states. Consequently, we can become conditioned to respond emotionally in the same way over and over again whenever we generate a particular thought or whenever a particular stimulus is experienced. You may vaguely remember hearing this from someone else: Pavlov, who got a dog to salivate simply by ringing a bell.

Our lives are full of anchors, some of which have powerful effects. The sight of the American flag or the sound of "America the Beautiful" inspires deep feelings of patriotism in some people. Seeing a snake or a spider can evoke intense fear in those who are phobic. The smell of popcorn stirs up just-right feelings that make Peter Carruthers, a 1984 Olympic pairs skater, skate his best. The thought of a past event—like skiing a particularly difficult trail successfully—can evoke the same feelings associated with it in the here and now.

Skiers have more anchors than the Sixth Fleet. Unfortunately, some of them are negative, similar to phobias. Merely seeing an icy patch, for instance, is enough to create intense anxiety in many skiers. The thought of skiing a black diamond trail can evoke discomfort in some people or arouse excited anticipation in others. Hearing the hum of a lift motor can give the shivers to those who have had spills getting on or off a lift. Entering the starting house is enough to get some slalom skiers anxious and tense.

Other anchors consist of some form of conscious, compulsive, and superstitious behavior. Superstitious anchors range from wearing certain pieces of jewelry or clothing for good luck to believing that adjusting the bindings of the left ski before the right will produce a successful run every time. And some Christian ski racers cross themselves as insurance against injury. Frequently, ritualistic behaviors interfere with the ability to generate the most appropriate state for protecting yourself from harm. Some skiers deliberately psych themselves up to ski a black diamond trail, only to discover later that it was entirely too difficult. A heightened state of false courage can prevent a skier from determining the demands of a particularly tough run.

On the other hand, metaskills anchors automatically evoke appropriate feelings for skiing well, without the need for conscious thought. They automatically utilize your talents and emotional states, enabling you to ski well consistently.

Retrieving Past Experiences

Let's see how we can use the Sherlock Holmes Exercise to retrieve past experiences so they can be anchored for practical use while skiing. In that exercise, you learned how to go inside your mind to retrieve or remember a past experience. You learned how to run your brain by modifying sights, sounds, and feelings. And you identified the condition or state of consciousness when your thoughts, emotions, and muscles conspired to have completed as fine a skiing maneuver as you had ever made.

This process of "going inside"—remembering what you saw, heard, and felt during a particular past experience—is, as I've said, central to practically all of my mind games. It's there, in your brain and muscles, that you have all the resources you need to ski as well as your physical condition and skills will allow.

Sherlock Holmes Revisited

Let's revisit the Sherlock Holmes Exercise as a way to learn how to anchor. Quickly reread the instructions on page 31. When you've finished reading, go inside and go back to that wonderful maneuver that you examined as Sherlock Holmes before. See, hear, and feel again what you saw, heard, and felt when you skied at that specific time. Be sure to make regular pictures, not meta pictures, because regular pictures elicit stronger feelings. Especially feel the emotions you felt *while* you were skiing. Pay attention to the bodily sensations of that emotional state. Perhaps it's a tingling feeling, goose bumps, warmth, a rush of blood, or a feeling of energy or power in some part of your body.

As you become aware of these sensations, press one finger against *one specific part of your body*. Increase the amount of finger pressure as the intensity of the emotional sensations increases; as the intensity subsides, reduce the amount of finger pressure. That's the anchor—a K-anchor—the pressure of your finger on a specific part of your body. The central idea is to associate the anchor with the emotion.

When the emotion is fully present, let one, and only one, internal image associated with the maneuver flash *spontaneously* into your mind; then let one sound associated with the maneuver pop *spontaneously* into your head. The image and sound are also anchors—a V-anchor and an A-anchor. They should be related directly and specifically to the past maneuver and not to skiing in general.

Now let your mind go blank and come back to the present. Take a five- or ten-minute break from reading this book and do something else to distract your mind from what you have been reading. At the end of the break, return to this point in the book.

Welcome back. Take thirty seconds to determine the nature of the state you're in right now. After that, press your finger on the exact same spot on your body as you did when you were Sherlock. Hold the finger pressure for a full sixty seconds without reading any farther than the end of this paragraph. Just pay attention to what happens inside, nothing else, and then return to the book when the sixty seconds are up.

Welcome back again. Are you thinking about the past good maneuver? Do you now see or hear what you saw or heard then? Do you now feel the same emotions you felt when you executed that maneuver? I'd be surprised if you aren't aware of some aspect of the maneuver, assuming you followed my instructions. If you reactivated some of the same feelings, images, or sounds associated with the maneuver, you have experienced how an anchor works. Within sixty seconds you changed your state.

Now reflect on the meaning of this experience. Do you realize that you can change your state quickly and therefore don't have to stay stuck in a lousy state? With a properly established anchor you have more choices about the way you want to feel, and you can activate any state automatically if your anchor is "contextualized."

Contextual Anchors

If an anchored resource is to be useful on the hill, it must be contextualized—that is, the anchor should fire *automatically,* without conscious thought, in the context of a special skiing situation when a particular resource is needed, not just arbitrarily. If anxiety normally takes over as you get on the ski lift, a confidence anchor could be triggered automatically just before you get in the ready position, awaiting the arrival of the chair. If you want to keep your cool as you approach a mogul, a calmness anchor could be activated automatically when you first see it. If a forceful edge is to be applied on a tight turn, the anchored feeling of lifting and turning the downhill ski could be fired automatically just before you enter the turn.

When you contextualize an anchor, it's important to select either a movement, an *external* visual cue, or an *external* auditory cue that is always present on the hill to serve as an anchor. Only one cue is necessary. For example, getting your pole straps adjusted on your wrists, a K-anchor, could be used to generate the resource of determination; looking at the tips of your skis, a V-anchor, could be applied to get into the right state for making a jump.

Your ingenuity is all that's necessary to identify an anchor. Using as an anchor a habitual, unconscious movement that invariably occurs in a particular situation or context is most effective, since it is already done without conscious thought. Habitual, unconscious movements could include the way you hold your poles, the manner in which you put on your gloves, how you lean on your poles as you wait your turn to go down the hill, or the way you adjust your goggles.

The only limitation on your choice of an anchor is that it be "clean"—not already associated with an experience on or off the hill. For example, looking at a wedding ring would not be a good V-anchor because it's already connected to very powerful emotional experiences.

Making Anchors Work Automatically

To establish these anchors fully so they'll be useful later, it's necessary to "fire" them consciously three or four times a day for a week or two, until the anchored emotional state is activated within a few seconds. The act of firing an anchor consists of deliberately looking at an external visual cue, or listening to an external sound cue, or moving in a habitual way while consciously associating the A-, V-, or K-cue with the actual emotional feeling of a resourceful state. After you are able to activate a particular emotional state quickly, forget about consciously firing the anchor. Just let the process drop into a form of automatic unconscious behavior.

If you would like to *establish* the finger-pressing anchor related to the maneuver that you identified as Sherlock, press your finger on the specific part of your body and consciously see the internal image and hear the internal sound that were part of the remembered maneuver. The finger pressure should be maintained until you feel the return of the full force of the emotional sensations you had while skiing. Repeat this process several times each day for the next week or two. With this anchor-firing practice you'll eventually be able to reactivate the emotional state associated with the past maneuver in a matter of seconds. Eventually the emotional state will automatically be generated whenever the cue is present, irrespective of your conscious awareness of it.

If you want to *contextualize* the anchor for that past good maneuver, select either a habitual movement, an *external* visual cue, or an *external* auditory cue that is always present *while you're skiing* to serve as a new, substitute anchor. Practice firing this new anchor three or four times a day for several weeks until it works as well as the finger pressure; this may be done on or off the hill. When you're off the hill, just think about the external cue or make the habitual movement until you can produce the emotional state in a few seconds.

One professional skiing instructor looks at the printed logo on her skis; it's her V-anchor for generating determination. Another skier feels the grip on his poles; this is his K-anchor to activate a state of confidence. A third skier listens to the sound of his skis on the snow as he approaches the start; this A-anchor activates a just-right feeling of excitement before the start of a race.

All of these skiers used finger pressure on some part of their body when they first identified and anchored their resource during the Sherlock Holmes Exercise. They fired the finger-pressure anchor on the hill to regenerate the desired state. Then they transferred the feeling anchored by the finger pressure to a new A-, V-, or K-anchor that is always present at the time they need the resource while skiing.

The skiers practiced firing these new anchors both on and off the hill. When at home or in the office, they imagined they were on the hill. Then they saw, heard, or felt their particular anchor and consciously generated their desired emotional state. After they were able to generate the desired state in association with a particular anchor within a matter of seconds, they stopped formal practice and allowed their unconscious minds to take over—just the way hearing a certain song can automatically generate a feeling of love for a special person.

ANCHORING

1. Identify the resource needed to achieve a particular desired outcome or to execute a particular maneuver.

2. Remember a past experience when you used that resource successfully.

3. "Go inside" and see, hear, and feel again what you saw, heard, and felt during that past resourceful experience.

4. Intensify the internal, emotional feelings that were present during (not after) the time when you were actively involved in accomplishing a particular outcome or executing a particular maneuver.

5. Anchor the internal emotional feelings or state with finger pressure and with an image and sound that were directly associated with that past experience.

6. Contextualize the anchor to a sight, sound, touch, or habitual movement that will always be present in the skiing environment.

7. Practice firing the anchor four or five times per day for about two or three weeks so that the internal, emotional feelings can be regenerated in a few seconds.

Now that you know how to anchor a resource with external cues, you'll learn the practical uses of anchors in subsequent chapters, using both external and internal cues.

Metaskills
Techniques

Now that you're aware of your mental detective skills—the tools of sensory awareness—you're ready to uncover your internal resources and apply them to improve your skiing. The metaskills mind games in this part of the book are designed to allow you to: (1) identify and stabilize in your mind and body the just-right states that make for confident skiing, (2) discover how to take advantage of the instructor within yourself, (3) expand your ability to use the power of self-hypnosis, and (4) learn how to control pain and speed up healing so you can ski at your physical best. In short, you'll be learning how to run your brain so your runs down the mountain are safe and satisfying.

Read through this section of the book leisurely. When you discover a technique that fits a goal you have in mind, put it to work. *Follow the instructions precisely.* Then evaluate the effectiveness of the technique by asking yourself this question: Did I achieve my outcome?

If you're not sure about the application of a particular technique, go to the last chapter, *"Après* Ski." This chapter, along with Appendix B, will help you select appropriate techniques to achieve your desired outcomes.

FOUR

Mapping the Territory: Preliminary Steps for Building Confidence

Square one in skiing is knowing the level of your ability and being able to match it to the difficulty of the hill. Tackling a trail that is beyond your capability is foolish, inviting a free ride to the bottom—horizontal on a toboggan.

This chapter deals with two major mind tasks: mapping your way down the hill, and readying yourself to meet new skiing challenges confidently. I will describe ways to *begin* to deal with fear and to create realistic courage to ski steep black diamond trails or race on rugged slalom courses. Specific techniques for actually breaking through fear are covered in Chapter Five.

Knowing Your Ability

Obviously, your ability to do anything is based on experience; the more you ski, the greater chance you have to improve your skills. But experience alone won't tell you how good you are and whether you should tackle a difficult trail. To know just how good you are can be based on what your instructor tells you *and* from information generated by your unconscious mind; both are useful. Rely on your instructor to tell you when you are ready to ski certain trails. He or she is familiar with the mountain and can assess whether you're ready for a particular run.

The Unconscious Mind as Ally

In addition to your instructor's assessment, you have a powerful ally available for making decisions: your unconscious mind! It can signal you in the form of discrete physical symptoms, internal images, or internal sounds when things are going right or wrong.

To prove this to yourself, remember times when you made two kinds of decisions: one that you knew, ahead of time, was right and it turned out right; and one that was iffy before you acted on it, and it turned out wrong when you did act. The two memories don't have to be related to skiing.

Pay attention to the internal A's, V's, and K's as you remember the decision-making process in each of those prior events. I'm sure you'll discover a distinct difference in one or more bits of sensory information that were present during the process of making the good and the not-so-good decision.

Some people have a feeling somewhere in their torso that lets them know when a course of action, such as skiing down a mountain, is okay or not. Others see distorted internal images or hear discordant sounds when it's not okay to do something. Some people have more than one signal. In addition, these same signals are frequently present in a variety of activities.

It is this kind of unconscious signaling that you can apply when making decisions about how to ski the terrain and whether you want to tackle challenging trails. Your unconscious mind will spontaneously generate *yes, maybe,* or *no* signals. These signals indirectly reveal the level of your ability. Honor them, because they are yours, unadulterated by your conscious mind. They represent your intuition. They can save you from harm or generate confidence when you face new challenges.

Mapping Your Route to the Bottom

All good skiers plan their routes to the bottom of a hill. Sometimes it is done quickly and automatically, without much conscious thought, especially on slopes that are easy. At other times it is done carefully and deliberately, to ensure a safe or a quick trip. This planning occurs *before* starting down the hill and *during* the trip when the entire run cannot be seen from the top.

To map a route on the trail ahead requires some fancy internal visualization, similar to the graphics that occur on television with multiple screens and camera angles. If you discover that you have difficulty with visualization, refer to the sensory-awareness exercises in Appendix A. With practice, you can become adept at creating the internal graphics needed to map the territory of the mountain.

"Zoom"

"Zoom" is a technique I developed after listening to Dave Hill, a Canadian Slalom and Giant Slalom skier, describe how he planned to ski what he called a "death-defying" run down a narrow chute in an out-of-bounds back bowl several years ago. That chute is now known as the Blowhole, a controlled run at Black Comb Mountain in Whistler, British Columbia. Dave is as exceptionally facile with his mind as he is with his skis, probably reflective of his interest in architectural engineering. Here's some of what he described.

As he looks down the chute, he "picks his points" where he plans to turn. In his mind, he charts his course on a screen two feet by one and one-half feet in size, located about one foot in front of his face; the screen is tilted perpendicular to the pitch of the terrain. He superimposes this internal visual chart of his route over his external view of the terrain ahead. Having the screen perpendicular to the slope of the run is most important because it helps him rehearse the proper forward or "attacking" position needed to ski well.

Then Dave uses his built-in zoom lens and brings an enlarged image of the first turn up onto his mental screen to replace the chart of the entire course. In his mind, he rehearses that turn with regular movies as he gives himself silent, verbal instructions on how to turn. If his movies are fuzzy, or if he doesn't feel comfortable making the imaginary turn, he rehearses it again and again with a new regular movie until he gets it right. If he still can't get a clear picture and comfortable feelings, he looks down the hill and picks a different spot at which to turn.

When satisfied with his mental rehearsal of a turn, Dave

zooms the image of that turning point back down to its place on the course and then zooms in the image of the next turning point. He mentally watches and silently talks his way through the entire run, turn by turn. When all turns are okay in his mind, he's ready to go.

When Dave skis an unknown trail that is not fully visible from the top, he stops on the hill before skiing the next section and consciously goes through his zoom technique. When he skis well-known slopes, his planning is not as consciously elaborate; he quickly notes where he will turn but he doesn't *consciously* use his internal screen and zoom lens; nonetheless, as Sherlock he discovered that his unconscious mind does.

A variation of this route-planning process used by other skiers includes making a large meta movie of skiing successfully down the mountain. The movies are of themselves, as seen from the top, following a line or path superimposed on the slope. The "zoom" technique is then used to plan each turn, using a meta or a regular movie.

En route Planning

Another way to rehearse a route is by using multiple images on a large mental screen *during* the run. The entire screen contains rapidly changing snapshots of the *planned path* from turn to turn all the way to the end of a section, or the bottom of the hill.

In addition, one corner of the large screen contains a series of separate regular or meta movies of the skier successfully making each turn nanoseconds before he actually turns. In other words, the skier superimposes a movie of making each turn onto the map of his run. This is especially useful when turns are initially out of sight at the time when advanced planning takes place.

The above description of en route planning sounds as if it's done consciously. It's not. The unconscious mind does most of the work, while only a few key thoughts are in conscious awareness. However, for the unconscious mind to be capable of en route planning, conscious practice of it is needed. To help you develop your ability to plan success-ful routes on difficult trails, practice the "zoom" until it can be done quickly and automatically.

"ZOOM"

1. At the top of the hill or at the beginning of a new section of a trail, identify the location of each turn-ing point.

2. Mentally plot a line on a mental screen from start to finish through each turn. Tilt the screen so it's per-pendicular to the slope of the hill.

3. Zoom in on the first turning point and mentally rehearse making the turn, using regular pictures. Tell yourself what to do and feel the action in your muscles.

4. Repeat Step 3 until you feel confident.

5. If not confident about making a particular turn, identify another possible turning point that could be easier or safer, and repeat Step 3 until you are confident.

---

6. If at any time you don't feel confident, then abandon the trail or ski cautiously. The turns that appear fuzzy on your mental screen or feel uncomfortable in your muscles are communications from your unconscious mind that you could lose control.

"Zoom" can be practiced at home in an armchair or on the way up in the lift. Just pretend you're looking down a trail and start the process. It can also be practiced while actually skiing on a very easy section of a familiar trail. With deliberate practice, the process will gradually become second nature and will be activated automatically at an unconscious level, just the way it is in the minds of expert skiers.

Meeting New Challenges

Almost every skier I know wants to ski better and to ski more difficult trails. To do this, it's important to "conquer" each beginner's trail with confidence before graduating to more difficult runs. Sometimes skiers feel pressured to ski trails that are too difficult. If they succumb to the pressure, they often end up fearful of skiing because their ability doesn't match the demands of the hill. Either they fall, are injured, or they suffer continuous fear as they make their way to bottom, feeling both shaken and embarrassed when it's all over.

Before you tackle a new trail, master the one you're now working on, especially the sections that are most troublesome, using both physical and mental practice. "Zoom," along with other metaskills techniques described in the next few chapters, will facilitate the development of consistency and confidence. When you can ski a trail well time after time, confidence follows. Let's see how we can build these two feelings.

What's needed are *specific* memories of having skied well. You can anchor these memories solidly so you don't forget them, especially when you come up against some difficult parts of a slope. Here is one metaskills anchoring technique that produces a genuine feeling of confidence based on skiing well consistently.

Skiing Resource Anchor

Bill, a recreational skier, built his confidence by accessing the just-right states for several kinds of specific maneuvers. He then anchored each of them to a specific movement of some part of his body that occurred naturally *just before* he started each maneuver.

Bill wanted to make his medium-radius turns more consistent on a blue-square trail he frequently skied. As we stood near the chair lift at the bottom of the trail, I told him to think about where and when he wanted to turn during an upcoming run. He was also to remember a past, successful series of similar turns on terrain roughly equal to what he would be skiing shortly. He had had many such experiences, so it wasn't difficult.

"I want you to *be very precise about remembering* and anchoring that past series of turns," I said. "See, hear, and feel again what you saw, heard, and felt then until you become aware of the emotional state you were in *while* you were turning, not the feelings *after* you completed them."

It took Bill a few moments, but then he said, "I've got it. I was just going with the flow, feeling free. I felt like I could do no wrong."

"How do you know you felt free?" I asked. "What sensations in your body let you know you felt free? Really pay attention to all of your bodily sensations, from head to toe, that indicate freedom."

"My chest was lifted, like I was standing tall, and my legs felt loose yet strong," Bill replied. "When I'm going with the flow, I'm always aware of these physical feelings."

"Before you anchor those feelings of freedom," I said, "let's do a prior mental test of their usefulness. Generate those feelings strongly right now, and in your mind ski down the trail here. As you ski in your mind, find out if your medium-radius turns go the way you want them to."

In this instance, Bill said his mental turns were just fine. However, if his mental turns had not been up to his required level of performance, he was to identify the emotional state associated with another successful experience of turning. Then he was to test that emotional state in his mind before anchoring it.

As Bill and I continued to work, I said, "Let's find a natural movement that you always make just before you start to turn. We'll use it as an anchor."

"Well," Bill said, "just before I go into a series of turns I automatically get my hands up and forward. Could that movement be an anchor?"

"Sure," I answered. "Let's use it. Here's what I want you to do. Get yourself into that feeling of 'going with the flow' and associate it with getting your hands up and forward. Actually move your hands up when the feeling becomes really strong. Then lower your hands and let the feeling subside. Do this a couple of times and condition yourself until you can't have one without the other."

Bill looked out into space as he thought about his "flow" feeling and slowly lifted and lowered his hands a couple of times. "I think it's anchored," he said.

"Temporarily, at least," I replied. "Let's see if it works on the hill." I told him to *prepare* mentally for his upcoming run *as he normally would* when he reached the top. I emphasized that he should plan his route as he always had. Then I told him to generate the feeling of freedom by raising his hands and to think about making the medium-radius turns *before* he pushed off. If he was satisfied that the turns in his mind were good, he would be ready to go.

"I want you to ski the trail without thinking about the turns," I said. "Just focus on the trail. When you get back here, we'll talk about what happened. Off you go."

When Bill returned to the bottom, I asked him to rate the quality of his medium-radius turns on a scale from 1 to 10, with 10 being perfect.

"They weren't perfect," Bill reported, "but they were at least a 7, and I really felt loose and free. It would be nice to ski that way all the time."

"Great. Do it again exactly as before, and let's see what happens."

When Bill reported that the quality of his turns on the next run was a 7-plus, it was clear that the anchor was working. So I told him to practice the anchoring process on and off the mountain three or four times a day for the next three weeks. "When you are able to experience the flow feeling within a second or two of raising your hands, no more practice is needed. Just ski without firing the anchor; it will gradually become honed to fire automatically. As a consequence, your unconscious mind will control your turns."

Later, Bill and I went through the entire anchoring process again, using different kinds of maneuvers such as poling on flat traverses, jumping over knolls, skiing through moguls, and stopping techniques. Bill created a *new K-anchor for each kind of maneuver:* putting his pole straps over his wrists as he prepared to start a run down a steep slope, riding an edge as he skied on ice, and getting into a crouch when he wanted speed. All of these anchors were natural movements that Bill normally made *during his preparation* for each maneuver. When we finished, I asked him what he had learned from the process.

"I learned I could recall past runs quite fast after I got the hang of it," he said. "When I anchored myself in the right state, I found I wasn't brooding over runs that I messed up the way I used to. I was too busy just skiing."

Bill had only one question: "When do I fire each of these anchors?"

"Only during practice, as you're building them," I replied. "The practice sessions will make them fire automatically since the anchor is a natural movement that you can't not make when you ski. You know, the way Pavlov's dog salivated when the bell rang."

"What if I'm faced with a trail that causes me to question my confidence and scares the bejingers out of me? What do I do then?" he asked. "Do I fire all of these anchors just before I go down the hill?"

"Hold the phone," I told him. "We'll get to that later. All we're doing now is working on each maneuver to make your skiing consistent. Developing a way to meet the challenges of steeper runs comes later."

The following is an outline of the steps used to create your own just-right anchors for various skiing maneuvers.

SKIING RESOURCE ANCHOR

1. When you're ready to practice a particular kind of maneuver (e.g., a turn, jump, or stop), remember a specific time and place when you had executed that maneuver well.

2. Go inside and see, hear, and feel again what you saw, heard, and felt when you were doing the maneuver. Remember the physical sensations *and* the emotional state you experienced *as you were executing it.*

3. Preliminarily test the usefulness of the emotional state. Generate the emotional state and mentally ski the maneuver. If you mentally ski well, you're ready to develop an anchor. If not, repeat Steps 1 and 2.

4. Anchor the emotional feelings with a unique and *natural movement* that occurs just before you start the maneuver (Bill used the raising of his hands as a K-anchor).

5. Test the effectiveness of the anchor on the hill. If you ski well, continue to use it. If not, repeat Steps 2–4 using a different emotional state and a different K-anchor.

6. Practice firing the anchor three or four times a day for three weeks—at home, in the office, on the mountain, wherever. By then, the anchor should fire automatically whenever you ski.

The same process can be used for any type of maneuver. When you finish, you will have about five or six different just-right resource anchors. If you later discover that a particular maneuver is becoming inconsistent, you can repeat the six-step process and create another anchor.

Bill and I spent a lot of time on the mountain building his just-right resource anchors. He had the luxury of time and money to practice. But what do you do if you're an occasional skier who is limited to perhaps one or two weekends of skiing per month? About all I can recommend is that you use the morning of the first day of the weekend for practice, leaving the rest of the time for just skiing. And, of course, you can use an armchair for mental practice several times per week between outings.

Competitive-State Anchor

For those involved in competitive skiing, there are times during competition when anxious moments unnerve even the most highly skilled. Often the anxiety erodes confidence in one's ability. Most skiers know when they lack confidence, especially at the starting gate and at crucial points on the course, because their ability to ski well goes kerflooie. Quick recovery from these periodic episodes of self-doubt is crucial to enjoying skiing and racing well. What's necessary is to be competition-keen and stay that way. An anchor can help you do this.

A competitive-state anchor can be created by skiing in your mind a complete and successful run on the night before or the day of a race. This means that you already have a race plan and know the nature of the terrain and location of the gates.

The idea is to make a fantasy run on the course, mentally executing as many different and difficult maneuvers that could occur during an actual race. As you mentally execute successful maneuvers, anchor the positive feelings generated during the fantasy race by stacking them into *one* anchor while you're mind-racing. The anchor can be an ordinary movement, such as stroking your chin, rubbing your arm, or pulling an ear.

If, in your mind, you mess up a gate, reski it mentally several times until it's okay. If a particular part of the course continues to be troublesome in your fantasy, never mind. Continue your mental race, anchoring the good feelings as you go along. After the race is over, you can correct the errant fantasy maneuvers during practice sessions. If they occur during the actual race, so be it.

When you are finished, you will have anchored (stacked) good feelings of confidence many times, and you will have mentally reviewed the course in advance. Practice firing this one competitive-state anchor several times until it generates confidence in seconds.

When you first arrive at the mountain, and as you approach the course, fire the competitive-state anchor. If you become overly anxious while in the starting house, fire it just before the countdown to put yourself in a better frame of mind.

COMPETITIVE-STATE ANCHOR

1. Fantasize skiing a specific racecourse.

2. Anchor and stack the confident feelings of skiing each gate well. Use a normal gesture as your anchor.

3. Practice firing the anchor until you can access your state of confidence within a few seconds.

4. Fire the anchor prior to the start of a race.

Personal Power

Skiing a successful fantasy race beforehand and anchoring feelings of confidence may not overcome more pervasive feelings of insecurity. Sometimes anxiety, manifested by stomach discomfort and headaches, starts hours or perhaps days before race day. Sometimes insecurity begins to gnaw at a skier's mind toward the end of a competition. If you haven't developed ways to cope with your anxiety, you may perform poorly at crucial times. Moreover, your feelings of insecurity can also affect other parts of your life, such as school, work, and social relationships.

There's a way, however, to tap your resources of powerful effectiveness and overcome anxiety. It's a process I've developed that keeps you in touch with your feelings of competence and confidence so you can perform comfortably at the peak of your capacity when the chips are down.

It's a personal power anchor—an anchor to be used sparingly and for only the most significant events in your life.

I hit upon this idea of anchoring personal power after thinking about what Carlos Castaneda wrote in his book *Journey to Ixtlan,* (New York: Simon & Schuster, 1972), on pages 181–89. Don Juan, Carlos's sorcerer, talked about the importance of being prepared to face fear and death gracefully and courageously. He said that each person should identify a personal place of power—an actual geographical place where he has experienced a sense of awe combined with exhilaration, strength, and confidence.

Whenever that person reaches a goal of utmost significance, he is to return to his place of power, either in actuality or in fantasy, and "deposit" the feelings of powerful effectiveness there. Then, according to Don Juan, when death approaches over his left shoulder, he is to return to his place of power, either in actuality or in fantasy, gather the deposited power into his being, and dance the dance of death—that is, face death courageously, replacing the feelings of fear with power.

Don Juan created a process to deal with death; I have converted it to deal with living. My process, the personal power anchor, consists of identifying your place of power, "storing" the feelings associated with your own experiences of being powerfully competent, and eventually tapping those resources of power when you're faced with events of utmost significance in your life, which are sometimes frightening or anxiety-provoking. Essentially the process is an anchor that you fire to empower yourself to make living full of rich experiences instead of anxious ones. Here's how it works.

Identify a Personal Place of Power

In your mind, go back to a specific time and place—a place that overwhelmed you with its beauty, where you were at one with nature and the universe, where you experienced a sense of excitement and confidence. That place may be close by or hundreds of miles away. It could be in the mountains, near a lake or the ocean, in the midst of a forest or a field of grass, under a majestic tree, next to a cool stream, in the rain or snow—no matter, just a very special place for you.

Go inside and see, hear, and feel what you saw, heard, and felt when you were in that place. Notice the light, shadows, and colors; listen to the pitch, volume, and tone of the sounds; and especially feel the sensations of awe, excitement, and confidence that you felt while in that special place. That special place is going to be where you, in your imagination, can "store" all the feelings you've had when you did things superbly, powerfully, and independently. It's also a place where you can eventually store all the feelings of powerful competence that you'll experience in the future.

Identify Past Experiences of Power

Remember and relive a time in your life when you performed a task, any task, superbly. Perhaps you felt a sense of graceful and easy power as you skied your very best. You might have felt extremely satisfied after giving a fine speech before a large audience. You might have been excited after completing a top-notch interview. You might have been really pleased upon being cast in a school or college play. Or you might have had a deep feeling of caring and love after writing a letter to a special person.

Relive that past experience of powerful effectiveness. See, hear, and feel again what you saw, heard, and felt then. See the things you saw on the inside—in your mind —and on the outside. Pay close attention to the submodalities; *most of all,* feel those physical sensations of powerful effectiveness and confidence.

Anchor the Powerful Experience with a K-Anchor

As a K-anchor, use a movement that is natural and unobtrusive, such as touching your face or making a fist. Associate the K-anchor with a special image and sound that are directly related to the past experience.

Create a Storehouse of Power

Fire the K-anchor, and when the feelings of power are strong, "deposit" those feelings in the one particular spot you have chosen as your personal place of power. In your mind metaphorically see that power stored there.

Increase the amount of stored power by repeating the same process with other past experiences of achievement. Continue to build your storehouse of power when you have similar experiences in the future. "Stack" feelings of power from each new experience into the *same* K-anchor.

Tap the Storehouse of Power

When you want to perform superbly in crucial situations, you can recapture the feelings of powerful effectiveness. Fire the K-anchor, go to your place of power in actuality or in fantasy, and see the imaginary storehouse of power. Do this several hours or the night before you want to perform at your very best. Remove as *little* power as necessary by metaphorically grasping a small portion of it in your hands. Actually reach out, "grasp" power, and then bring your hands to your chest until you feel confidently energized.

PERSONAL POWER ANCHOR

1. Identify your geographical place of power.

2. Identify a past experience when you performed at your very best.

3. Anchor the physical sensations of powerful effectiveness with a natural, unobtrusive gesture (K-anchor), a special image, and a special sound or word.

4. Go to your place of power, in actuality or in fantasy; fire the K-anchor and metaphorically "deposit" the feelings of power in that place.

5. For each past and future experience of power, repeat Steps 2 through 4 and stack the feelings of power associated with them in the same K-anchor.

6. To tap your storehouse of power when you're faced with a very important task, fire the common K-anchor, go to your place of power in actuality or in fantasy, and see the storehouse of power that you deposited there. Do this the night before or several hours before you want to perform at your very best.

7. Take as *little* power as necessary and bring it into your body until you feel confidently energized.

Now that you know how to map your runs down the mountain and understand how to identify and anchor a variety of just-right states, let's turn to learning how to overcome the most prevalent emotions faced by all skiers: *doubt* and *fear.*

FIVE

Just-Right State: From Doubt and Fear to Confidence

Undeniably, fear has rattled and ripped the confidence of skiers the world over, if only for seconds, and sometimes for years. Fear skips no level of skiing competence. Beginners and world-class skiers alike experience this barrier to enjoyment and achievement. Those who perceive it as a challenge to overcome, like Liisa Savijarvi, a Canadian World Cup skier, usually advance their skiing ability, recapture the enjoyment of being on the mountain, and certainly expand their self-esteem.

Liisa, ranked second in the world in Super G and fourth in the world in Downhill in 1987, openly described how she overcame a "huge fear" before and during a Downhill race. Liisa said: "I spent the whole night and the whole next morning worrying about it. On the street looking up at the mountain I was saying, 'I don't want to do this.' " This continued until seconds before she poled out of the starting gate. While in the start house she was hearing the rattling sound of skis on the icy course and was thinking about an accident that occurred the day before. She was still saying to herself, "I don't want to do this. I'm going to kill myself."

Just before the five-second countdown, Liisa dramatically changed her internal state from intense fear to aggressive determination. She went from being thoroughly confused and doubtful to knowing she could ski successfully. "One second I was looking all around the starting area and saying, 'What are you going to do? Your skis are too fast. You should have done something about this last night.'" In the next second, she became focused on the course and the clock and said to herself, "I don't have the guts to quit. The only way I can get out of it [her fearful, nauseous state] is to do it [ski down the hill]. I'm going to do it." At this point, she thought about skiing well, standing tall with her hands up and forward. In her mind, she was hearing the sounds and feeling the rhythm of successfully turning through the gates on the first section of the race-course.

During the actual countdown, Liisa started to tell herself reassuringly what to do. "Liisa, keep your hands up and forward. Liisa, if you push yourself, you'll be fine. If you stay aggressive, Liisa, you'll be fine. You better be so bloody aggressive or you're going to kill yourself. Get your hands up and go for it."

Afterward, Liisa said she was scared all the way to the bottom of the course. She just kept saying to herself over and over again, "Get your hands up"—a phrase that, for her, embodied the elements of skillful skiing. She ended up in ninth place, by far her best result to that time. Upon reflection, Liisa told me, "When it came down to the crunch, I wasn't gutsy enough to walk away from the race and face the embarrassment of chickening out. One fear overrode the other. That race was a turning point in my career."

I hope you, too, will be able to think of fear as being useful for protecting you from taking undue risks. Fear can serve as an anchor, believe it or not, to trigger a just-right state for skiing well.

The Anatomy of Fear and Confidence

A skier's fear, as you probably can imagine, is essentially a fear of serious injury or death resulting from falling or crashing into obstacles. Fear is initiated either by the thought or act of losing balance and control. The paradox of skiing well without undue fear is deliberately to go with gravity. In other words, skiing consists of falling upright, not in a heap, down the mountain. This, as good skiers know, means becoming part of the mountain slope with its powerful gravitational pull. When fear creeps in, the willingness to become part of gravity wanes; as a result, performance deteriorates. How does this come about?

The V's, A's, and K's of Fear

When scared, skiers invariably experience a sense of urgency to do something quickly, and they experience what seems to be an unusually rapid passage of time. Their perception of external reality is frequently restricted to tightly focused awareness of a "danger" immediately ahead that looms much larger than it normally is. Their internal screen is dominated by repeated meta pictures of imagined "doom," such as hitting a tree, slamming into the billy bags, or tumbling forward over their skis.

Sometimes they remember scenes of others who have fallen on the trail or racecourse ahead of them. Or they relive past accidents in their minds. They reexperience the pain and hear again the voices of the medical personnel who treated them.

No wonder they lose control or have second thoughts about going down a tough new trail. No wonder they feel weak, break into a cold sweat, become covered with goose bumps, and get dizzy. Their fearful thoughts activate the autonomic nervous system and put them into a lousy state that precipitates even more doubt and fear.

Most skiers in jeopardy on the hill are aware of being unbalanced and extremely stiff and tense. They have little or no feeling of their skis on the snow, and they grip their poles for dear life. All of these K's make for uncoordinated, jerky movements—exactly what is not wanted. Further, they make things even worse when they silently and harshly criticize themselves. Some also begin to debate with themselves about what to do next.

You would normally say these thoughts and sensations are totally useless. On the contrary, they can serve as signals for you to think positively rather than negatively. The trick is quickly to be able to sense and trust the very first discomfiting sensation so you can immediately change your thought processes. If not, your fantasy images of doom could become a horrible reality.

A little bit later, you'll learn three simple techniques— "Stop," "Flash," and "Breakthrough." These techniques are used to interrupt and change negative and fearful thought patterns in a second or two. Before doing this, however, let's continue with descriptions of the mental structure of confidence.

The V's, A's, and K's of Confidence

As in fear, there is also a consistency and commonality of mental activity when skiers are confidently in control. Some of this mental activity is conscious; a lot is out of awareness. Skiers in control are automatically engaged in perhaps the most useful form of mental activity needed in time of danger, or at any time while skiing, for that matter. They are repeatedly making visual and kinesthetic comparisons between what is going on in the here-and-now and what they know from similar past experiences. They see images, for example, of making a turn coming up and compare them with pictures of successfully making similar turns at other times. They constantly compare the ongoing mechanical feelings of skiing properly with feelings they experienced during successful maneuvers in the past.

The internal images of confident skiers invariably consist of either two movies on a split screen, or two alternating movies, as described previously on pages 59 through 63. One of the movies portrays the remaining portion of the planned route to the bottom of the hill; in this movie (regular pictures) the different snow conditions along the way are sharply defined. The movies of the route have extensive depth of focus, yet are wide-angled.

The other movie (regular pictures) depicts, up close and personal, the way the execution of their very next turn will look (and feel) like. These turning movies are usually bright, sharp, and tightly focused, as if the skier is actually at the place where the turn is to be made.

Matthew King, an expert skier, used an interesting mental process of getting back into control when skiing too fast on a trail at Vail, Colorado. Not only did he have a meta movie of himself stopping to regain his control, but he also yelled to himself, "Brakes!" At that point he created another meta movie, superimposed on the first. In it he saw himself tossing three or four anchors attached to ropes back up the trail to take hold and slow him down.

Internal auditory representations of skiers who are confidently in control usually consist of assertive, short commands or words of praise such as "weight forward," "hands up," "good work," "great," "go for it." Instead of hearing their own voices, some skiers hear music, its rhythm matching that of their turns.

Kinesthetically, skiers in control frequently experience bodily feelings of warmth and lightness. They grip their poles loosely; stand tall; and, of course, have an exquisite feeling of their skis sliding over the snow.

Barriers of Fear

Many skiers talk about fear indirectly, referring to it as a barrier. Amy Hill described it this way: "I have a barrier [when skiing a transition over a knoll into a steep pitch], not knowing what's on the other side. Even though I've gone over knolls thousands of times, I always pull back." Amy broke through her barrier one day when she was free-skiing a challenging Downhill racecourse at Aspen.

I had Amy become Sherlock Holmes to discover how she mentally overcame her fear. As she was skiing the Aspen course, she said she saw, as she approached a knoll, ". . . light at the end of the tunnel . . . an aura of vibrant blue around a bright, white light" that replaced the darkness of the trail just beyond the knoll. This common, light-at-the-end-of-the-tunnel metaphor encouraged her to risk unweighting her skis as she prepared to enter the transition into a steep pitch. As Sherlock, she discovered that she also had an internal snapshot of her desired outcome —the bottom of the hill. Upon reflection of this experience with me, Amy recognized that the white light with blue border was a metaphor that represented her just-right state for skiing well on all sorts of terrain. She had seen this light at other times while skiing well. She labeled this state *contentment.* By being in this state and having an internal image of achieving her outcome at the same moment, Amy was able to break through her barrier.

In a different vein, Chris Parrot, a highly skilled skier, thinks of dangerous challenges as "boundaries." He used the term "tremendous anxiety" to label the boundary he experienced when he first got back on skis after he had recovered from a serious skiing injury to his knee. He overcame that anxiety while skiing the Liniwey trail at Arapahoe Basin, Colorado. He said, "In my mind I pierced through an easily shatterable surface that broke into very small pieces." He explained that he took a risk to unweight his right ski and move ". . . up into the gap of being momentarily out of control between the end of one turn and getting into control of the next turn, which required using my previously injured left knee." As Sherlock Holmes he discovered that the impetus for taking this risk was an unconscious, composite meta picture—a picture of having entered that gap of being momentarily out of control many, many times before, when he skied well.

Other skiers have had similar barrier-breaking experiences. All involved having a distinct, internal image that represented a definite positive outcome. And all of them conquered their fear in a fraction of a second. For example, to break through his fear of skiing the Paradise Headwall at Crested Butte, Colorado, Jerry Beilinson saw an instantaneous flash of an instructional book on skiing. That flash immediately shifted him from anxiety to confident determination to conquer the Headwall.

Allison Hobart, while skiing Porcupine at Mad River Glen in Vermont, broke through her barrier of fear of skiing on ice by consciously changing her internal movies. While skiing fearfully out of control, she realized that she was making internal meta pictures (slides) of herself making jerky turns. As soon as she shifted to creating regular pictures of having skied competently on ice before, she immediately regained her confidence and told herself, "Do it!" And she did it, successfully.

"Breakthrough"

The "breakthrough" technique, described below, is designed to help you overcome fear quickly while skiing a difficult trail. The idea is to condition your brain to make positive, internal images *automatically* whenever you have even the slightest feeling of unbalance or lack of control.

''BREAKTHROUGH''

1. At home in an armchair think about a certain kind of maneuver that usually frightens you when you get out of control on the hill.

2. In your mind, see yourself from behind (either a meta movie or a series of meta slides) losing control while doing the maneuver on a familiar trail; feel a loss of balance in your body.

3. Construct a regular movie of skiing correctly, keeping it in your awareness until you feel balanced and controlled. Make sure your mental screen is in front of you and tilted so it's perpendicular to the slope.

4. Imagine yourself (using regular pictures) breaking through an easily shatterable surface (e.g., gauze, Saran Wrap, paper, whatever).

5. Repeat Steps 2, 3, and 4 *rapidly* until you can break through your barrier and shift from loss of control to control in two seconds. Let your mind go blank between each repetition.

6. Go to a beginners' hill and allow yourself to get *slightly* out of control while doing only one kind of maneuver. Be prepared to fall if necessary.

7. As soon as you are aware of being out of control, repeat Step 5 until you can regain control instantly. The positive image of controlled skiing should accompany the image of shattering a barrier, with no delay between the two whatsoever. When this happens, stop practicing. It's in there!

8. Repeat Steps 6 and 7 for a variety of maneuvers that are anxiety-producing.

9. Put the technique to the ultimate test. Ski a trail that matches your ability, and find out what happens *automatically* in your mind if you should happen to lose control. If you don't lose control, you've already mastered the once-dreaded maneuver.

Letting Your Mind Go Blank

A surefire way to get yourself scared is to think about fearful possibilities by making scary pictures of them. A surefire way to overcome the coldness of fear is first to let your mind go blank and then replace the scary thoughts with positive ones. The nature of a blank mind can be different for different people. Some, as they say in television lingo, go to black. Others see white, like a snowy, pictureless television screen.

Here is a two-step way to run your brain so that your mind can shift to positive thoughts:

1. "Stop." The four-letter word *stop* works wonders if you want to eliminate horrible thoughts. Whenever you're thinking negatively, just say to yourself, *stop.* Let your mind go blank and then shift to a pleasant or positive image. If you're a doom-and-gloom person, it'll take some practice saying *stop* to interrupt the worry program you've already grooved in your brain.

2. "Flash." Some people find it hard to let their minds go blank after they say *stop.* But all is not lost. Just pretend, for a moment, that you're about to have your picture taken by a photographer holding a flash camera. Then, in your mind, see the flashbulb light up. What happened to your vision? If you're normal, you have a lasting image of bright white light, period. Your mind has gone blank, *and* you have stopped thinking about whatever you were thinking about. Your mind is now ready for positive thoughts.

Meeting Challenges on the Mountain

Practically every skier I know wants to ski better and conquer more difficult trails. What usually stops them are thoughts of crashing. To overcome these fears, a number of skiers have repeatedly asked me how they can mentally prepare themselves to meet risky challenges. The Challenge Process described on page 95 is a technique that evolved from querying expert skiers about how they prepared to ski a really tough run.

Here's how the Canadian SL and GS skier David Hill prepared to ski the Soudan Couloir at Black Comb Mountain in British Columbia. The Soudan Couloir is known as one of the steepest and most radical runs within a controlled skiing area in North America.

The entrance to the start of this run is guarded by a chain link fence with ominous warning signs communicating danger and caution. The Soudan Couloir is strewn with lots of huge boulders and has four or five cliff drops of ten to twelve feet each on the way down. The initial part of the trail approximates the slope of one of the World Trade Center towers. Dave said if he could have stood just under the starting point he would have been able to lean back into the hill. Now, that's steep.

Advance Planning

Dave started to think about skiing Soudan Couloir three weeks before he actually skied it. His thought processes are instructive for understanding the Challenge Process described on page 95. Although Dave's planning was extensive and methodical, most of it was done automatically by his unconscious mind, out of his awareness at the time.

He realized, after we dug into his unconscious mental processes, that he prepared for most of his other skiing challenges in the same way.

Dave's initial thought processes consisted of watching himself ski the imagined Soudan Couloir run. His internal pictures of the trail were based on his friends' verbal descriptions of it. His internal movie consisted of dim pictures of the trail but clear meta pictures of himself in color skiing rhythmically and successfully. His view of himself was from the bottom looking up the yet-to-be-seen mountain gorge. While doing this he felt the action of his muscles and had a positive rush of adrenaline. This confirmed in his mind his original statement to his friends, "I'll have to try that." His motivation to do it, he said, was to experience the "pure satisfaction" of having met a really tough challenge.

During the three-week period before his trip to Black Comb he periodically thought about skiing Soudan Couloir. He created the same kind of movie as before, watching himself zigzag down the mountain. With each movie, he became increasingly aware of the physical feelings of making successful turns. This, he said, increased his confidence each time.

During his flight from Toronto to British Columbia for the express purpose of skiing the Soudan Couloir, Dave thought at least three or four times about skiing the trail. Again, he made meta pictures of successfully skiing the trail, feeling his muscles working as he watched.

Getting Ready

At breakfast on the morning of his first attempt to ski the trail, he repeatedly (about eight times) thought about making the run in exactly the same way as before. This time, however, he felt more excited about the possibility of meeting his challenge than at any time before. He said that he felt strong, as if "I could take on the world." In his mind he kept saying to himself, "I've gotta go do that."

It takes three chair lifts to reach the top of Soudan Couloir. While riding the first two lifts, Dave anticipated what the run would look like from the top looking down. He wondered if it was like other challenging runs he had skied successfully, such as Walsh's Run at Aspen and KT 22 at Squaw Valley. His recollection of these two trails consisted of replaying a regular movie of what he saw when he had successfully skied them. All these recollections generated muscular sensations of skiing that increased his excitement and confidence.

While riding on the second lift, he became ambivalent. On the one hand, he thought positively about how he could physically and mentally prepare himself to make the challenging run ahead. He silently told himself to take several preliminary warm-up runs of lesser challenge on Black Comb to ". . . build my confidence, get good feelings of skiing well, and then go hit this other one"—the Soudan Couloir. He also built his confidence by recalling successful runs on familiar hills at home.

On the other hand, Dave started to doubt. He wondered if he could make it down the Soudan Couloir in as smooth and rhythmical a manner as he had pictured earlier. He felt cold inside and lost the feeling of strength and tension in his legs that was needed to ski well. Not until he actually saw the hill did he relieve himself of doubt.

Mental Test Runs

When he reached the top of the second lift, Dave finally saw the Soudan Couloir from the bottom up. He immediately changed his original, internal meta movies of himself coming down the run, by making his images of the terrain accurate and sharper. His new test-run images of himself coming down the trail became much more narrowly focused, and his mental screen was smaller and closer to him than before. These movies of himself increased his excitement and reduced his doubt.

After he made several mental "test runs" on the Soudan Couloir, he compared them to having successfully skied Walsh's Run and KT 22. Whenever a test run was deficient —when it didn't compare favorably to his other actual runs —Dave would metaphorically reach into a bag of mechanical skiing tools and pull them into the movie to make his mental test runs better. Some of his mechanical tools included riding an edge, steering by pressing the balls of his feet, and moving his weight forward to feel the front of his boots on his shins. When his test-run movies were completed, he said they looked like a "visual montage" of different kinds of past, successful skiing experiences tied together into a complete movie of skiing the Soudan Couloir.

Warm-up Runs

After completing his mental test runs, Dave took two warm-up runs on reasonably easy trails nearby to prepare his body and build his confidence. While skiing down these trails, he ran through a mental checklist of the mechanical aspects of skiing necessary to ski well. He also compared his ongoing performance with feelings of past, successful performances on his home mountain, fine-tuning mechanical adjustments until he felt competent and confident. At times he would deliberately make incorrect maneuvers, then correct them so he felt confident of his ability to adapt to conditions that might throw him off balance. David said, "I get a quick shot of the bad and then the good feels that much better."

At the end of the first warm-up run, he mentally reviewed it by comparing images and feelings of what he had just done with the remembered images and feelings of doing them well at his home mountain. When Dave discovered elements of his performance on the first warm-up run that were less than adequate, he told himself to make certain corrections on the next. He felt compelled to make them because of the demands of the Soudan Couloir.

On the way back up on the second chair lift, Dave visually compared, in his mind, his performance on the first warm-up run with his prior mental montage of skiing Soudan Couloir, noting which of the maneuvers on the warm-up run didn't match the montage. In this way, Dave identified the skills he needed to fine-tune during the second warm-up run. All the way up on the chair he kept telling himself to improve certain maneuvers and to ski the best way he knew how.

At the end of the second warm-up run, Dave reviewed his performance, noting that everything was working well. He said to himself, "Okay, keep it this way now" as he looked at his internal montage of skiing the Soudan Couloir. When he saw that he was mentally skiing the Soudan

Couloir well, he lost most of his doubt and said to himself, "Now I gotta go do this."

Approaching the Challenge

Up he went again on the second lift. He made sharper mental movies of himself skiing the Soudan Couloir while on the way up and when he saw the bottom of Soudan Couloir again. These movies consisted of seeing himself skiing down the trail as if he were looking up from the bottom of the hill. On the third chair lift to the top of the mountain, Dave began to feel some of the coldness and weakness of doubt creep in. He still didn't know what the run looked like from the top down. All of his mental movies up to this time had been seen from the bottom up. So he decided to construct a wide-angle, fuzzy snapshot of what he guessed the Soudan Couloir would look like from the top down. The snapshot pictured the location of the boulders and other elements of the severe terrain he had seen earlier.

Upon reaching the top, he skied over to the fenced-in entrance to the Soudan Couloir, still unable to see the run until he got inside. When he finally looked down the run, Dave experienced what he said was a "little fear"—weakness in his legs. The pitch was steeper and there were more and bigger boulders than he had imagined previously.

He managed his fear by saying to himself, "This can't be so bad. It's in a controlled area." To support this conclusion, he had compared the slope of the Soudan Couloir with each of the slopes of Walsh's Run and KT 22 individually. Dave superimposed internal images of each of those trails on top of the Soudan Couloir and concluded that the slope in front of him wasn't as steep as the other two. He also ran internal regular movies of having skied the two other trails successfully. Taken altogether—the overlaid images and the sights and feelings of having skied tougher runs successfully—Dave felt strength return to his legs, and his confidence level started to come back up. So he said to himself, "Oh, I can do this!"

Planning and Executing the Run

Dave planned his route as far as he could see down the gorge, using the "zoom" technique described earlier, on page 60. When he finished zooming, he felt as confident as he had felt on the warm-up runs. This, he said, was equivalent to his just-right state when skiing at home. Dave no longer had any doubt. He gave himself "an extra boost" by saying, "Do it the way you pictured it, and let's see what happens." Just before starting down, he checked his posture, balance, and muscle tension. Since they were just right, he said to himself, "Away we go!" And away *he* went along with the other part of him—his trusted unconscious mind.

Dave successfully completed the first section of the run as planned. At the end of the section he stopped and mapped the remainder of the run. At the bottom of the hill he felt exhilaration, exclaiming, "That was all right!" Since he hadn't fully met his challenge to ski the entire run without stopping, Dave immediately returned to the top. While on the lift, he reviewed his performance. Then he made a new regular movie of going down without stopping. This, he said, increased his confidence.

When Dave stood at the top of the Soudan Couloir the second time, he felt neither fear nor doubt. In his mind he "zoomed" the entire trail again quickly, feeling stronger, the way he usually felt while skiing at his home mountain. After a final physical check of his feet, legs, stomach, and hands, he said, "Okay, let's go." He went all the way down —faster, smoother, and without stopping. He commented to me saying, "I had really beaten up on it."

When Dave and I finished examining how he prepared himself to meet a tough challenge, it became clear to both of us that the most crucial parts of his preparation consisted of repeatedly making internal movies of his expected performance; feeling the muscle sensations of skiing while making internal movies; accessing complete memories of having successfully skied similarly difficult trails; warming up and making sure his skiing mechanics were working properly; constantly comparing internal images and feelings of past successful runs with what he was doing either in his mind or actually doing on the hill; accepting *and* resolving any doubts about his ability to meet his challenge; getting into a just-right state of strength, tension, and confidence before skiing the Soudan Couloir; and making sure that all his thoughts ended up completely positive. All of this eliminated any chance of recklessness or injury.

Here is a synopsis of the Challenge Process:

CHALLENGE PROCESS

1. Identify what you want to accomplish—your desired outcome—and make a clear meta movie of actually doing it successfully. It's okay if the movie is not completely clear.

2. For several weeks, continue to run the meta movie a couple of times a day. Be sure to feel your muscles moving as you watch your private rehearsal.

3. Early in the day before you attempt your challenge, repeatedly make your internal movie (from Step 1), but change it to regular pictures when you know precisely where you will be skiing. Make sure your private show is clear, sharp, and distinct; actually feel your muscles moving as you mentally ski.

4. Make regular movies of having done something similar and equally as difficult as your challenge. From this you will be able to generate feelings of confidence.

5. Make regular movies of having skied successfully on familiar runs at home, making sure you feel confident and experience your just-right state.

6. Ski several warm-up runs to prepare yourself physically. The idea is to tune up your skills and feel confident and competent enough to achieve your outcome. If doubtful about your ability to meet your challenge, repeat Steps 3 through 6, making corrections in your skills when necessary.

7. Go to the trail where you will achieve your outcome; plan your route to the bottom, seeing clearly in your mind (regular pictures) what you want to accomplish.

8. When you feel confident and have successfully achieved your outcome in your mind, ski down the hill, doing what you had planned to do in Step 7. If doubt remains, repeat Steps 3 through 7 until you feel confident. If not, reconsider the value of trying to achieve your outcome.

9. When you get to the bottom of the hill, evaluate the quality of your performance. If satisfied, you've met your challenge. If your performance is not up to your expectations, make any adjustments necessary in your mental movie from Step 3.

10. Repeat Steps 7, 8, and 9 until you're satisfied with your performance.

Now that you have some ways to make use of your doubt and fear to help you gain confidence in your skiing ability, the next step is to learn how to put yourself into a state that lets you ski well consistently. The next chapter focuses on getting into that state, called the "zone."

SIX

Just-Right State: Getting into the "Zone"

I'm sure you have experienced at least one run during which you felt as if you were one with the mountain, free of pressure and tension, skiing with effortless control, and having tons of fun. Many people refer to this kind of state as the "zone." One of my clients described her zone as a Zen state: ". . . a light, ghostly feeling, as if the wind could go straight through me instead of slowing me down. . . . Light, like you don't feel you're touching the snow. . . . I don't think I left a mark even though I know I did." Another client describes the zone as feeling weightless and experiencing an auditory resonance reproduced as a vibration throughout his body.

Jerry Beilinson describes his skiing zone poetically. "I capture the feeling of grace in movement which brings my mind and body together with the quiet wilderness. It's like falling in a controlled way, a smooth, graceful way of moving very fast, faster than I can under my own power. It feels like a dolphin swimming. Skiing brings about a feeling of liberation from the ordinary feelings of my body. . . . Skiing is like dancing, which allows me to express my emotions through the way I ski. . . . And powder skiing is just fun—a childlike feeling—jumping into the deep, fluffy stuff, like jumping into a huge thing full of Styrofoam balls." How delightful his experience is.

When a skier is in the just-right state of mind, he seems to ski mindlessly. When this occurs, mind, mood, and movement are solidly melded, with all control left in the hands of the unconscious mind. A sense of harmony in the skier's body produces rhythmical and effortless turns and jumps. His attention is riveted on each maneuver, yet there is no conscious concentration. He feels as if he's in another world or in a trance, which, indeed, he is.

Some skiers report that any sense of urgency is eliminated as time seems to slow down in the zone. In this state it seems as if they are executing their maneuvers in slow motion.

This chapter focuses on the use of color, music, and images to produce satisfying skiing, sometimes resulting in the creation of the "zone" state. The descriptions of metaskills techniques that follow are designed to distract the conscious mind from deliberate thought about the mechanics of skiing so the unconscious mind can do its natural work of controlling the trip down the mountain almost effortlessly.

Skiing with a Colored Image

You may remember a young women I introduced earlier in the book, Amy Hill, the Canadian junior skier who used an image of a "puffed pink balloon" to get into her zone of contentment for skiing. Here's how Amy worked with me to create this colored-image anchor. The anchor was designed to help her be more consistent when skiing transitions from a flat section over a knoll onto a steep pitch.

Using the Sherlock Holmes Exercise, Amy recalled how her mind controlled her best-ever free skiing on a Downhill course at Aspen. She discovered two important things. First, she felt extremely light and loose. Second, she realized that her feet were exquisitely attuned to the terrain. Amy said it was astonishingly easy for her to ride a clean edge, then release, roll, extend, and dive into a turn at just the right instant. And when she landed it was silent as she touched the snow and rolled over to ride an edge. She said, "I wish I could ski that way all the time."

"Let's do some things," I said, "that will make it possible for your brain to control that kind of skiing more often. Tell me what your emotional state was like then."

"Sorta out there somewhere," she answered. "Just like being with the day, skiing, and that was it. I was very content."

"When you're skiing your best, what do you always do physically with your body *just before* you go into a transition?" I asked.

"Release pressure of my edge, roll flat, and then extend up and forward."

"Great. Let's use part of that movement as a K-anchor to get you into that state of contentment." But first, I instructed her, "Get yourself back on that Downhill racecourse when you felt so content. See, hear, and feel again what you saw, heard, and felt then until you really feel content. Just nod when you get that feeling."

Within less than thirty seconds, Amy nodded. "Now I want you mentally to associate that feeling of content with the release of the pressure of your edges on the snow so that the two feelings come together simultaneously."

After about a minute Amy looked up and said, "I've got them coming together at the same time. It's like taking a breath of air that brings them together."

"Now," I asked, "how could you chunk the release and roll and contentment together metaphorically? Let any kind of crazy image pop into your mind as you do it."

"A pink balloon," she said after a moment of thought. "And that's what it's like. It sort of comes up and then floats down. It's like putting a puff of air into the balloon, and it fills up more."

"That metaphor seems to fit your complete description of skiing the transition nicely—releasing and lifting lightly into the next turn," I remarked.

"Yeah, it really does," Amy agreed.

"Let's see if this works, at least in your mind, right now. Go inside and mentally ski another transition section of the same Downhill course. When you're finished, come on back here and tell me what happens."

Amy closed her eyes and mentally skied the course again for about a minute. "It's very clear, actually," she said. "The balloon was down on the center of the hill, and each turn was as if I jumped right around it."

"And how was your performance?" I asked.

"Oh, it was good, really good. But I had to alter my image of the balloon before I got it to work. Initially it was a meta picture of me and the balloon. The balloon was too predominant and the picture was too far away. So then I changed to a regular picture. I saw the balloon on the trail ahead; but when I came to the point where I planned to turn, I only saw a big balloon as I released and rolled and dived around it. After that I saw the trail ahead and another balloon at the next turn."

"Okay, that's one positive test of the balloon image," I told her. "But we need to find out if this V-anchor works on the hill. The next time you ski, go to an easy run. While skiing, do exactly what you just did in your mind here. When you get to the bottom, immediately rate the quality of your skiing. If you're satisfied with your performance, you have a good anchor.

"Make sure it works at least three or four times before you practice making it become automatic. Assure yourself that every time you fire the anchor the quality of your skiing satisfies you. If not, we'll change it."

"How can I make it automatic?" she asked.

"Just go to other sections of the hill, fire the V-anchor— that is, see the pink balloon—get the feeling of contentment, and note the quality of your skiing. You can also practice firing it three or four times a day at home or at work. Whenever you're bored, just practice."

At this point Amy asked, "How will I know if the anchor has become automatic?"

"One day you'll be skiing a transition well, and without even thinking about it that puffed pink balloon will appear on your internal screen. When that happens, it's automatic. It's in there. No more conscious practice is needed."

Eager to know how the anchor would work on the hill, I asked Amy to give me a call to let me know what happened on her next ski trip. Several weeks later she called, saying that while skiing a chute at Whistler, she saw lots of puffed pink balloons popping up automatically on the trail. She said, "The balloons took me to an inner calm and I skied with such ease and relaxation."

COLORED-IMAGE ANCHOR

1. Using the Sherlock Holmes Exercise, remember a specific time when you skied superbly. Pay attention to how you felt emotionally while you were skiing so well. Identify the emotion with a word or phrase such as "determined," "relaxed," "excited," or something else.

2. Identify a particular kind of terrain and snow cover with which you normally have difficulty.

3. As Sherlock again, remember a specific time when you skied a section of a run that matched the terrain in Step 2 really well. See, hear, and feel again what you saw, heard, and felt then. Identify the mechanical aspects of skiing that you executed during that run, feeling the movements that made the run so good.

4. Pick one of the movements identified in Step 3 that is most essential for skiing that terrain well. It may, for example, be how you plant your poles, how long you ride an edge, or how you release the pressure of your skis.

5. In your mind, pretend to ski a particular section of a specific run that is usually difficult. In your mind, chunk the emotional feeling identified in Step 1 and the movement identified in Step 4 together. (Amy chunked the feeling of contentment with releasing her edges.) Make sure they come together in your mind simultaneously. If you ski the imagined run well, you've selected a good K-anchor. If the imagined run is a bad one, repeat Steps 4 and 5, selecting another movement to chunk with the emotion until you get a successful imagined run.

6. Mentally reski the difficult trail with the chunked anchor in mind, allowing any colored image whatsoever to flash onto your mental screen spontaneously, without conscious thought. (Amy had a pink balloon.)

7. Mentally reski the same difficult trail with only the colored image in mind. If you ski the imagined run well, you've generated a good V-anchor. If the imagined run is a bad one, repeat Steps 6 and 7 until you get a colored image that makes the imagined run successful.

8. Mentally practice skiing two or three difficult sections of familiar trails several times a day with the V-anchor in mind until it's easy to do.

9. Go to the mountain and prepare to ski a difficult trail. On the way up on the lift and just before going down, mentally ski that trail a couple of times with the V-anchor clearly in mind.

10. Ski the trail three or four times, seeing only the V-anchor on the way down. If the runs are successful, the anchor is a good one.

11. Continue firing the V-anchor three or four times a day, on or off the hill, for a couple of weeks until it becomes automatic. Then just ski; the colored image should flash into your mind spontaneously.

Confidence Anchor

Not too long ago, Kristin Larkin, an intermediate skier, wanted to improve her stem christie turns and feel confident doing them. Working at Hidden Valley in Vernon, New Jersey, I asked Kristin if she had ever done them well. She had, a couple of years before in Colorado, while working with her instructor. This is how we proceeded to improve her turns and increase her confidence in her skiing ability.

Before having Kristin ski, I instructed her to go back in her mind to when she had had a lesson with her instructor in Colorado. "Pay attention to how you felt," I told her, "while you were doing stem christies really well."

"I felt very light, yet solid and grounded in my center," she replied. "It was a feeling of confidence."

Then I asked Kristin to construct an image of that feeling. She described it as a solid, square box that encompassed her lower torso with vertical lines connected to her shoulders.

I also asked her if she had ever felt exactly that way before during her life, at times unrelated to skiing or to sports in general. She recalled a time when she was playing a part in a workshop production of a play, *Shadowland*.

So I had her go back to the workshop production and find out if that feeling of confidence while acting was, indeed, identical to the feeling of confidence while skiing. Kristin assured me that it was.

Then I had her pretend to ski a trail at Hidden Valley, using only stem christie turns. I told her to think only about *Shadowland* and the solid square with lines connected to her shoulders. She was to find out how well she executed stem christie turns. After a minute or so, Kristin reported that her mental skiing was successful.

Finally, I prepared Kristin to actually ski the Hidden Valley trail. I told her to say the word *Shadowland;* see the solid square with lines connected to her shoulders; and experience the feeling of confidence while riding on the lift. At the top, she was to repeat this process until the feeling of confidence became strong. I told her to ski down the trail when she felt confident, thinking only about the image of the square and connecting lines.

I queried Kristin about the quality of her skiing after each run. She rated her first run a 5 (with 10 being perfect); the second a 6; and the third, fourth, and fifth runs were 7s, satisfactory for Kristin. During one of the latter runs she modified her image by adding connecting lines from the central box to her feet and ankles. This, she said, made her feel as if her entire body was grounded.

On her sixth run she independently decided to add a waltz-time tune to match the rhythm of her turns, reporting that the quality of her skiing was now up to an 8. She was really pleased. (How she used music is explained in the next section of this chapter.)

"Do you feel like trying another more difficult trail, but one that's still within your range of competence?" I asked.

Excitedly, Kristin said, "Sure, I'm ready," and up she went.

When she returned to the bottom she blurted out, "I went so fast and I eliminated fear."

My response was, "Yea!" as I clasped and shook my hands overhead. I asked Kristin to continue to reinforce her mental anchor by saying *Shadowland* until she could generate the feeling of confidence in an instant while seated in an armchair. I also instructed her to use the

V-anchor (the box with connecting lines) on her pending ski trip with her husband to Taos, New Mexico, the next week. She was to do exactly as she had done at Hidden Valley: say *Shadowland,* see the image, and feel confident while riding the lift and just before skiing down the hill.

Upon her return from Taos, she called and said she had really increased her confidence level, even though she had fallen unexpectedly on an unseen icy patch. After her very first run on an advanced slope, her husband said, "Gee, Kristin, that [her confidence anchor] really worked."

After her fall on the third run, Kristin said it took her two more runs to get her confidence back. Furthermore, she said she became even more confident as she skied harder trails with *Shadowland.* She also reported making considerably more and faster progress with lessons taken at Taos. She was assuredly pleased with her skiing.

What excited her most of all was the elimination of her fear of flying on the flights to and from Taos. Normally she had been quite nervous about flying, taking a low dose of propranolol before each flight. Now she says that she takes no medication and is no longer anxious before or during flights. She approaches air trips like her skiing—confidently, thinking of *Shadowland.*

This kind of fundamental change in Kristin's level of confidence frequently results when any person makes changes in scary aspects of athletic performance. This is because the emotional states and strategies that regulate one form of a particular person's behavior are often the same states and strategies that regulate a variety of behaviors. You, too, can look forward to unexpected changes in behavior, like Kristin's.

Here are the steps you can follow to build a confidence anchor for yourself:

CONFIDENCE ANCHOR

1. As Sherlock, remember a time when you were skiing confidently. Pay attention to what that confidence feels like in the muscles and organs of your body.

2. Create a mental image of what the feeling of confidence looks like. (Kristin had a box with lines connecting to her shoulders and feet.)

3. As Sherlock, remember a time, unrelated to skiing and sports in general, when you had *exactly* the same feeling of confidence as you did while skiing. (For Kristin it was acting in a play.)

4. Generate the feeling of confidence while riding the chair lift, and again just before going down the hill.

5. Ski down the hill thinking of nothing except the mental image created in Step 2.

6. Rate the quality of your skiing on a scale from 1 to 10. If you ski satisfactorily at least three or four times, you have a good V-anchor.

7. Practice firing the confidence anchor (the image) on and off the hill three or four times a day for a couple of weeks until the feeling of confidence is generated automatically. Then just ski without any thought whatsoever. The contextual anchor will take over without any need for more conscious thought.

Music and Skiing

Early in my coaching career years ago, I noticed that athletes became transformed when music was played in the practice arena. Music seemed to change the rhythm and power of their movements. So I decided to investigate how all kinds of athletes use music to enhance their performance. Consequently, I developed a technique—the M & M Process—to integrate music and movement. This process, described in detail a little later, consists of having athletes select music that elicits or reinforces a just-right mood or state for performing well. Their movement, mood, and the music become all of a piece. As a result they move into a "zone" and play more consistently.

Since most runs down the mountain consist of a series of rhythmical turns, and since most skiers turn at a comfortable tempo to control their speed, it makes sense to use music to create a just-right state for both. Let's see how one skier used music to enhance his performance.

Using Music to
Maintain Turning Tempo

Lynn Gilbert, an expert skier and a professional ski instructor, wanted to be able to execute short-radius turns on the fall line comfortably, without fear. When I asked what stopped him from doing it, he said, "I have so much pressure on my brain." With questioning, I discovered that the "pressure" he felt was the result of talking to himself about how to turn while he was turning.

Many skiers, like Lynn, have developed the habit of giving themselves silent, verbal instructions while skiing. These instructions can be okay *before* going down the hill, but there's nothing more disruptive to the unconscious regulation of the complex act of skiing than internal talk *during* a run. Talking about what to do while skiing is much too slow. It causes confusion and loss of control. It's no wonder that Lynn was having trouble.

I asked Lynn to remember making a good series of short-radius turns and to listen to their rhythm. Then I told him to search his mind for a tune that matched the rhythm. Within a few seconds he "found" one. It was the Beatles tune "Hey, Jude." After two runs down the hill at Bellaeyre Mountain, New York, singing "Hey, Jude" to himself, Lynn had achieved his outcome. Several weeks later, Lynn said he had skied his best ever on a trip to Utah. He also said he would encourage his students to use music as a way to relieve the pressure of fear.

The M & M Process

The M & M Process is a systematic way of using music to regulate rhythmical turns. It consists of matching the tempo of turning with specific kinds of music. Here's how to do it.

Sitting in an armchair at home, become Sherlock and remember a specific time and place when you skied in a smooth, rhythmical way. See, hear, and feel again what you saw, heard, and felt then, paying close attention to the sound and feeling of the rhythm and effort that characterized that run down the hill. Then listen to different kinds of pleasant music that you think will match the turning tempo of that run.

It's important to match specific elements of music with specific parts of your turns. The elements of music consist of pitch, harmony, tone, rhythm or beat, volume, and intensity or "energy." The parts of your skiing that could be matched with the music might include: pressure of your feet on the skis, the length of the turn itself, speed of turning, building up pressure before releasing, planting your poles, and the force of the release.

For example, the rhythm of an entire piece of music, or even one musical phrase, might match a series of turns; a pause or an extended note could regulate the amount of delay you might want in order to build up enough resistance before releasing into the next turn. The energy or loudness of one song might be appropriate for the amount of force created by the release, while quite the opposite level of musical energy might be more suitable for making a soft landing after a jump. A quiet ballad might be just right for smooth, wide-radius turns, while Bruce Springsteen could be more fitting for attacking short-radius turns on the fall line of a steep slope. The possibilities for "matches" between music and skiing are infinite, especially if you want to match your existing mood to the way you ski a particular trail.

Now back to your armchair exploration. After an initial match of certain music with specific parts of skiing, mentally reski the previous run with the music playing. If the images of the remembered run are clear and positive, and if you can hear and feel your turning synchronized with the music, you've got a just-right match.

Now it's time to test it on snow while skiing on an easy hill. Take several runs while listening to the selected music, using a Walkman, or simply hearing a tune in your head. When you're satisfied that the music positively influences the tempo and effectiveness of your skiing, you have a good A-anchor.

While listening to the music in your mind, take several practice runs daily, making sure that the music and your turning movements match. Continue this practice until the music automatically comes into your awareness while you're skiing without thinking about music. If you can't ski regularly each week, you can still practice the same things mentally. Merely imagine you're skiing and let the music play in your head.

Keep in mind that it's quite possible that music could disrupt your concentration and interfere with skiing well. I recall working with one skier who became distracted by deliberately playing music in his mind while practicing Telemark turns on the hill. It seems that he had already established the proper turning rhythm to match his mood and turning speed by merely listening to the rhythmical schussing sound of his skis on the snow. When he listened to music instead, he shut out the sound of his skis and became distracted. The result: He fell. When he stopped the music, he skied much better. So the M & M Process, which is described here, may not be appropriate for you.

THE M & M PROCESS

1. Sitting somewhere comfortable at home, recall making a run; or relive a section of a trail you just skied. See, hear, and feel again what you saw, heard, and felt then, paying particular attention to the rhythm and effort of your turns.

2. Identify several pieces of enjoyable music that you think might have the intensity, beat, rhythm, and harmony that match either the entire action of your body or only a part of it.

3. In your mind test the match between the music and your movement. If the images of the remembered skiing experience are clear and positive, if you can feel your muscles contract and relax in harmony with the music, then it's time for on-hill tests.

4. Strap a Walkman to your waist and listen to the music while skiing down an easy hill. If you don't have a Walkman, hear the music in your mind.

5. If the run is good, play the musical anchor at home and while practicing on other trails for two or three weeks, or until the music plays automatically in your head while skiing.

6. Evaluate the effectiveness of the music periodically. If the quality of your skiing decreases, change the music.

Time Distortion

I'm reasonably certain you have noticed that time seems to pass quickly or slowly depending on your mental activity. If you've been speeding on the highway on the way to the mountain, for example, it's likely you'll feel tense while skiing. That feeling could disrupt your mental processing to the point that your mind races. As a consequence, you could ski too fast on the first couple of runs, endangering yourself. The same effect of time speeding up can result from feeling anxious about skiing a new trail.

Conversely, your body and mind might feel sluggish and tired. As a result, your turns could lack crispness and your timing could be slowed down. Time itself seems to slog along, with each turn taking forever to be completed.

What is needed to get your body and mind synchronized with your optimal skiing rhythm is a modification of your perception of time. When time perception slows down, your sense of urgency decreases and your coordination improves. Then your skiing performance can return to its normal level of effectiveness.

While working with some figure skaters in Sun Valley several years ago, I stumbled onto two very simple procedures that affect the perception of time and the timing of coordinated movement, such as spinning in figure skating, twisting in diving, and making medium-radius turns in skiing.

One of these techniques, the Counting Process, may remind you of the childhood game of hide-and-seek. You remember. When you were "it," you had to hide your eyes and count to 100 or some other high number. It seemed to take forever. Another, the Off-Ramp Technique, relates to the dramatic change in the sensation of speed when you leave a high-speed highway on the off ramp; then time and speed seem to slow down. One or both of these techniques will probably be useful if, for example, you want to slow down or speed up your turning rhythm. Experiment with both techniques to discover which is better for you.

The Counting Process

This metaskills technique merely involves counting, *first very slowly, then as fast as possible*. Count silently to *10* as slowly as possible. Then count silently to *10* as quickly as possible, to *20* as quickly as possible, to *40* as quickly as possible, and finally to *50* as fast as you can. Don't skip any numbers, the way you might have when you played hide-and-seek. After you've finished the counting tasks, immediately ski a section of a trail appropriate to your level of ability, paying close attention to the tempo of your turns. The result will probably be the exact tempo you want, whether it was too fast or too slow before you counted. This is because your perception of time has been altered and counting has distracted your conscious mind. Distracting your conscious mind lets your unconscious mind regulate the proper timing, faster or slower.

The Off-Ramp Technique

This technique consists of mentally traveling in an automobile on a superhighway at maximum speed while watching the rapidly passing center-line markings and seeing the light poles and trees peripherally, by the sides of the road. Listen to the hum of the engine and the *whoosh* of the wind as your car speeds along. Feel the vibration of the wheels through the chassis on your feet and the movement of the steering wheel in your hands.

Now imagine it's time to leave the highway as the exit ramp suddenly appears a very short distance ahead. Apply the brakes and hear the tires scrunch as they grab the road. Feel your body being thrust forward as you quickly slow down to thirty-five, twenty-five, and fifteen miles per hour in seconds. At this point the car will seem to be crawling along to the end of the ramp.

When this mental process is complete, immediately ski a section of a trail. The result will be a correction in the timing of your turns, either slower or faster, depending on what you're working on at the moment. Again, by distracting your conscious mind from the task of tempo regulation, your unconscious mind can do its natural work unimpeded.

The point of the past three chapters has been to help you get into the just-right states required for superb performance. You have probably discovered that some of the techniques are more attractive and useful than others; so be it. Now we can turn to learning how to run your brain so you can be your own instructor, acquiring new skills or relearning old ones.

The Pro Within: Your Instructional Mind

When you want to refine your skiing technique, you have two experts to call on for help: a professional ski instructor and your own mind. Both are important. You need a professionally trained instructor to teach you proper skiing mechanics. You also need to pay attention to your internal instructor—your unconscious mind. Believe it or not, it's this part of your mind that can help you coach yourself.

This chapter contains techniques you can use to correct your mechanics and to know the difference between how you run your brain when you're skiing well and how you run it when you're not. You'll also learn how to improve mechanics that are rusty and how to develop new skiing maneuvers without professional instruction.

Backup Process

Even expert skiers are not quite sure which elements of a skiing maneuver they want to refine. The Backup Process is designed to uncover them. It will also make your practice sessions more efficient. Here's how it goes.

Rehearse in your mind an anticipated run, noticing any obvious mistakes you might make. Subtle defects in your performance will be revealed by unclear images, garbled and discordant sounds, and uncomfortable feelings. Each distorted sensory representation identifies a specific part of a skiing technique that needs attention.

You may notice, for instance, blurred images while making certain turns or while skiing specific sections of a racecourse. You might feel unnecessary tension in your legs as you ride an edge; or you could hear an internal buzz as you prepare to jump. These specific internal A's, V's, and K's are all signals from your unconscious mind, telling you to refine the specific elements of the skiing mechanics represented by them.

After you know precisely what to practice, go to work and refine your skills, testing them on the hill when you're finished. If you're not satisfied with your performance, repeat the process to identify the elements still in need of refinement. When finished, test them on the hill again.

In sum, the Backup Process takes you from mentally skiing an anticipated or future run or race, back through practice sessions that prepare you to ski the best you can. The process teaches you to rely on your unconscious mind so it can help you identify certain elements of your skiing technique that stand in the way of achieving your desired outcome. In other words, the Backup Process activates your internal instructor, letting you know something about your skiing ability that you didn't know you knew.

THE BACKUP PROCESS

1. Go forward in your mind and ski a difficult trail or racecourse. See, hear, and feel all that you would expect to see, hear, and feel as you mentally ski the run.

2. Note the maneuvers of your mental run that are represented by incomplete, fuzzy, discordant, and uncomfortable sensory data. These distorted representations identify the specific parts of your skiing mechanics that need improvement.

3. After you have identified the subtle errors or weaknesses, refine them through practice.

4. When your mechanics are refined, test them on the hill. If your performance is good, you're finished. If not, repeat the Backup Process to determine precisely what you now want to correct.

The Difference That Makes the Difference

Many skiers are habitually inconsistent when they execute certain skiing maneuvers, and they can't figure out how to refine them. I have found that the way a skier mentally processes very small bits of sensory information while skiing determines whether he will ski well. The instructor within yourself can identify the differences in the bits of information that regulate a good and a not-so-good performance. When the differences are known, you can change the way you run your brain by deliberately using the difference in sensory information that makes the most difference in the quality of your skiing. Sometimes, although not always, this form of mental correction is all that's necessary to get yourself back on track, skiing a maneuver consistently well.

One day I was working with Howard Adriace, a certified PSIA ski instructor who wanted to improve his Telemark turns. I had him remember, as Sherlock Holmes, two different times when he had executed his turns—once superbly, once poorly. After his detective work, Howard discovered several important differences in the way he processed sensory information. They included: a tight focus on the trail ahead for the good performance and a wide-angled focus for the bad; hearing a quiet, rhythmical schuss of his skis during the good performance, and an arrhythmical sound of his skis on the bad; no internal imagery whatsoever during the good performance, and an array of negative "short subjects" of himself skiing poorly on his internal screen during the bad one; and a soft, encouraging internal voice during the good performance, as contrasted with a loud, shrill voice admonishing him for how badly he was skiing.

When Howard practiced his Telemark turns on an easy hill, he varied his internal mental processing by using only one of the submodality differences at a time. He wanted to determine which difference affected the quality of his skiing the most. Although the use of several of the differences improved his skiing, one stood out as more effective than the rest. It was the volume of his internal voice. Merely by keeping his internal voice very low, he was able to hear the rhythmical sound of his skis on the snow. When unable to hear them over his shrill voice, he sometimes fell. The sounds of his edges were crucial for him to maintain his balance and control. When the external sounds of his skis were overridden by his loud voice, Howard skied poorly.

A review of my notes of a dozen or so other skiers with whom I've worked indicates a variety of sensory differences that make the difference in successful skiing. They include bright, crystal clear pictures of successfully making each turn; absolute internal silence; an internal screen set at an angle of ninety degrees to the slope of the hill; a confident tone of short, positive statements of praise or instruction; rhythmical music matched to the tempo of turning; side-by-side, matching, or mismatching images of present and past performance; a single, bright, stationary image of being at the bottom of the hill; feeling the body centered in the lower abdomen; feeling the balls of the feet steering the skis; loose shoulders; flexible ankles; relaxed hands held forward and up; and lightness of the entire body.

Here are instructions for determining the mental difference that makes the difference between good and bad skiing. The basic idea of this metaskills technique is to find only one small bit of sensory information that, when concentrated on, will elicit good performance.

DISCOVERING DIFFERENCE

1. Identify two different runs during which you used a particular maneuver. On one run the maneuver was performed superbly; on the other it was terrible.

2. As Sherlock, relive each run separately, making notes of both the external and internal auditory, visual, and kinesthetic submodality representations that were involved in the two experiences.

3. Compare each of the sensory representations to determine their differences in nature and content. For example, pictures might vary in focus or brightness, sounds might vary in volume or tone, and feelings might vary in intensity or location in the body. (See Appendix A for information about your sensory systems.)

4. Select one of the submodality differences and incorporate it into your thought process while practicing the maneuver in question on an easy slope. Use the difference that regulated the past, bad performance first; this should result in another bad performance. Then apply the difference that regulated the past good performance; this should result in a good performance. Repeat this two-part process three times to determine the consistency of the effects.

5. Evaluate and compare the quality of the two performances. If there is little or no difference in qual-

ity, you can conclude that the submodality difference has little effect.

6. Repeat Steps 4 and 5 for each of the other submodality differences.

7. Compare the effects of all of the submodality differences with each other. Note which of the differences makes the most difference in the quality of
your performance.

8. When you are not skiing well, incorporate the submodality difference that makes the most difference
into your thought processes. This should result in
improved performance.

Developing a New Technique

After you have developed the mechanics of steering, turning, slowing yourself down, and stopping, it's natural to
want to learn new techniques that require skills beyond
the novice level—such as Telemark skiing, jumping, skiing
moguls, and different forms of turning. In addition, for
those who have had to lay off skiing for a season or two, it's
important to get back some of the skills that inevitably
were "lost" in the interim.

I've developed two metaskills techniques to help you
refine your skiing techniques by yourself—the Get-It Process and the Get-It-Back Process. These have proven very
useful, not only to skiers but also to athletes in many
different sports.

The Get-It Process

Roberta Warfield, a neighbor and a certified ski instructor, wanted to learn how to do royal christie turns in both directions well; she could only turn to the right. The person she wanted to model was a dear friend of hers who did them beautifully. Roberta had been attempting them by herself on and off for a few years, but never got beyond a quality level of 4 (10 being the maximum).

Having always been interested in doing things royally, I suggested that we work together, first in my office, and then on the mountain. Here's how Roberta and I worked together for about two hours to get a series of royal christie turns fit for a queen. We spent most of that time inside Roberta's brain figuring out how she ran it when she skied well. She spent about thirty minutes actually on the hill, skiing. When she finished, Roberta assessed her turning ability at a quality level of 9, a clear indication of the power of the mind to improve performance.

During the first part of our first session together, Roberta became Sherlock Holmes and reskied in her mind a time when she had done a royal christie as well as she had ever done it. As she described what she saw, I realized that Roberta was actually doing the Get-It Process (which is described in detail on page 129) without knowing she was doing it. So instead of teaching her to do the process, I merely identified to her what she was doing and what else she could do to refine her royal christie.

The way Roberta wanted to do royal christie turns was based on a remembered image of a very good friend doing them almost perfectly, ". . . with such grace," she said. Associated with this image of her friend was a feeling Roberta remembered while doing an arabesque in a ballet dance class years ago. This feeling consisted of relaxation (an absence of tension and stiffness) in her legs, back, and shoulders, and flexibility in her ankles.

Roberta also remembered her friend's behavior during a boring clinic several years ago. To add some humor to the clinic situation, her friend demonstrated a royal christie, a move that in itself is a bit humorous. When Roberta thinks of this incident it helps her, she said, "stay relaxed and not so intensely concentrated and visually focused on doing the turn."

After listening to Roberta talk about the royal christie, I decided to capitalize on her past experiences. So I said, "Let's play ballet. Pretend you're doing a royal christie to the left while watching yourself in a ballet mirror as you move down the hill. See yourself in the mirror doing the royal christie to the left. Can you do that?"

"Hmm-hmm," she said quietly.

"What you now see in the mirror as you're turning left," I said, "is what you will actually do when you turn to the right.

"Experiment in your mind with turning to the right based on the mirror image, and tell me what happens."

"It's not as good," Roberta replied, "but I didn't fall."

"Okay, now slip out and watch yourself from behind doing what you just did, and notice what parts of the turn you want to correct."

"I want to lift my left leg higher," she said.

"Stay out there watching yourself lift it higher as you move to the right. Does it get better or worse?"

"It gets better."

"Now slide into that picture; be there doing it," I told her. "What does it feel like?"

"*Much* better," she replied.

"Let's go back to the Sherlock Holmes Exercise; tell me what you heard on the inside as you were doing the royal christie."

"I heard myself talking about all of the specifics that needed to be in place for it to come off well. But when I do things well in succession, such as several turns, I don't talk very much. I just say, 'one, two, turn' to a waltz tempo, and tell myself to keep my hands up and forward."

"When you do things well," I reiterated, "you remind yourself to turn by counting to a specific musical rhythm. But when you did the royal christie in your mind just now, you had a bit of a dissertation going on in there, eh?"

"Yes," she agreed.

"When you practice the royal christie on the hill, I want you to eliminate as much of the talk as possible. Put some music in its place. Internal, silent talk is much too slow to be helpful."

"I agree with that," Roberta said. "But I also think it's helpful for me to say several key words, such as 'rise and steer.' That's all that's needed. If I say too much, I overload myself and don't ski well."

"As you refine your ability to do the royal christie, I hope you'll be able to limit your internal talk to zero, or to whatever minimally you need to say to turn well."

"I can already think of a word that would work," Roberta interjected. "Just 'shwoosh' would probably be the perfect word."

"Great," I exclaimed. "Take that one word out to the hill this weekend and see if it'll work for you."

At this point I gave her some instructions for practice. "Just before doing the turns on a safe slope, get yourself into a relaxed state by seeing your friend as she introduced humor into the clinic setting. Then practice the royal christie turn, refining only one part of it at a time. For example, first pay attention to the free-leg position, then the arm position for balance, then posture. Second, see an internal image of yourself superimposed on an image of your friend doing the royal christie as you practice the turn. And finally, do the mirror-image exercise as we did here a couple of minutes ago; but actually do it *while you're skiing.*

"Then, when you sense the images, feelings, and voice tempo come into your awareness automatically, stop the conscious mental practice and just do the turns without any thought. Merely say 'shwoosh' rhythmically, and maintain a wide-angle focus on the trail ahead. When we get together on the mountain in a few days, I'll help you refine the process so you're consistently able to reach a quality level of at least 7."

A week later, Roberta reported that she had skied over the weekend and was already doing her turns at a quality level of 7. She said it got better because she had spent so much time talking with me about the specifics of the turn during the Sherlock Holmes Exercise.

Even though she had achieved her outcome, we decided to work on snow at Belleayre Mountain a couple of weeks later. When the time came for practicing on the mountain, I instructed Roberta to practice the royal christie mentally while riding on the lift, and once more just before she skied down the hill. The mental practice was identical to the routine we had established earlier. While skiing, she was merely to say "shwoosh" and maintain a wide-angle focus down the hill.

At the end of the first run on a steep trail, which she evaluated as a "7," I had her make a movie of what she had just done and compare it to a remembered image of her close friend's model performance of the turn. "As you look at those two movies, identify one—and only one—thing you want to correct to make your performance become as good as your friend's turns."

Roberta looked out into space, where she projected two side-by-side images and said, "On the turn to the left I want my arms to be loose; on the turn to the right I want my free leg to be stretched out straight."

"What images spontaneously come to mind that could serve as metaphors for the loose shoulders and straight leg?" I asked.

Roberta thought for a moment, laughed, and said, "I see myself in a bathing suit where my arms feel free and unbound. And I also see a rubber band stretching."

Jokingly I replied, "Are you sure you won't be frozen stiff skiing in a bathing suit? Go ahead and visualize those two metaphors superimposed on a movie of making several turns right now, and tell me what happens to the quality of your performance. Do you loosen up and straighten the free leg?"

"Sure, it's fine," she answered after mentally reviewing several turns on her internal screen. "And I added a spoken phrase, 'Loosen up.'"

"Okay, off you go," I said, pointing to the chair lift. "See those metaphorical images and hear that phrase in your mind on your ride up and just before you come down. Then just push off and ski without any further thought except 'shwoosh.'"

When she returned to where I was waiting at the chair lift, she said she was "really pleased" with the last run, since she was able to see her shadow while doing the turns. She rated her performance an "8." On the third and last run, she did even better, giving herself a "9."

I said, "Mission accomplished. Are you satisfied?"
"Absolutely."

The Get-It Process

This technique is based on the element of mimicry and the fundamental process of constantly making mental comparisons between what you're actually doing and what you want to do ideally.

THE GET-IT PROCESS

1. Identify a time when you observed a fine skier execute a maneuver you want to learn.

2. On an imaginary screen, run a movie of that skier making that maneuver.

3. Put yourself into that movie, wearing your own skiing gear, and feel the movements involved in executing that skiing maneuver.

4. Change the meta movie into a regular movie and feel the movements of skiing well.

5. On an easy section of a safe slope, execute that maneuver. Evaluate the quality of your performance. If you "get it," repeat it several times a day for several weeks until it becomes automatic. If

you can't get on the mountain, just imagine it mentally as if you were skiing on snow.

6. If you don't "get it" (and most people don't the first time), make a meta movie of your last attempt and compare it to the original criterion movie in Step 2. Identify the muscle and joint actions needed to make the correction, and change the movie of yourself until you're doing the maneuver in your mind as well as you can.

7. Execute the maneuver on the hill several more times while paying attention *only* to one desired correction from Step 6. If the maneuver is satisfactory, you're finished. Practice it for the next few weeks in your mind and on the hill until it becomes automatic.

8. Many skiers don't "get it" even after a second try. In that case, go back and make another meta movie of your performance and compare it again to the Step 2 original. Ask yourself what *one and only one other* correction should be made. Identify the physical feelings that are necessary to make the additional correction.

9. In your mind, visualize doing the maneuver by "chunking" the two corrections (from Steps 7 and 8) together. Chunking facilitates concentration on making only one correction instead of several.

10. Execute the maneuver on snow several times more, paying attention *only* to the chunked correction. If that works, *you really are finished.*

Using Metaphors

Metaphors can be created to anchor the result of the Get-It Process. Here's how to create a metaphorical anchor.

---

1. After you identify a correction, create a metaphorical representation of it. (Roberta created an image of herself in a bathing suit and saw a stretched rubber band.)

2. Execute the maneuver several times while paying attention to the metaphor *only*. If your performance is satisfactory, the metaphor becomes the anchor.

3. If the first correction is made but the maneuver is still unsatisfactory, visually compare it to the criterion and identify another correction. Make a metaphorical representation of this second correction.

4. Visualize skiing by "chunking" the two corrections into one metaphor. If the maneuver is satisfactory, the chunked metaphor becomes the anchor.

Although it's helpful to create metaphors when correcting your skiing maneuvers, it's not absolutely necessary. Whether you make metaphors depends on the ease with which you generate them and the degree to which they facilitate or hinder your progress. For these reasons you can be flexible in the way you approach the use of metaphorical images.

The function of a metaphor is to quiet your conscious mind so your unconscious mind can do its work without interruption. All of the neuromuscular action that is necessary for skiing well is unconsciously associated with the metaphor.

Get-It-Back Process

The steps of the Get-It-Back Process are the same as for the Get-It Process. The only difference between the two is the identity of the person in the first movie (Step 2). Instead of the skier being someone else, it's you. It's you executing a skiing maneuver in the past that you want to get back.

Holographic Viewing

Holographic viewing is a systematic process of imagery that registers your observation of a proper skiing technique in your neuromuscular system, in the brain-nerve-muscle connections that make a skiing maneuver happen. It consists of watching a good skier from different positions "around the clock"—that is, watching him or her on the hill from the front, back, sides, and from above if possible.

Holographic viewing is quite precise. Immediately after you watch a skier execute, say, a turn, close your eyes and make an internal movie that reproduces the skier turning. Consciously feel your muscles become active while looking at the movie. When you're reasonably certain your internal movie accurately reproduces the skier's turn, move to a different position and watch the turn again. Make another internal movie and feel the turning action in your muscles as before. Repeat this process until you have seen your model skier make the same kind of turn from various positions "around the clock."

Now you have a set of criterion movies of a turn that you can match in the Get-It Process described earlier. Not only do you have a model to copy, but also you have already put into your brain much of the neuro-muscular activity you need to reproduce the desired technique. Many people have told me that by just passively observing skiers on the hill or on TV for several hours, their skiing improves on their next outing.

The metaskills techniques described in this chapter can be used for any kind of skiing maneuver; they will be particularly useful in developing new ones. Putting yourself into Alberto Tomba's place as he's racing an SL course may not put you in the Olympics, but it's worth the effort to improve your skiing.

Self-Hypnosis: Tapping the Power of Your Unconscious Mind

Athletes in many different sports have told me their best performances occur in states that are absolutely mindless. When competing, they just do it. Furthermore, without any thought whatsoever, they frequently know when a performance will be good even *before* they execute it. I'm sure this has happened to you, too.

These high-performance states are essentially trances that make it possible for the unconscious mind to control performance without interference from the conscious mind. The characteristics of high-performance states in skiing vary from person to person, as described earlier when skiers are in their "zone." The essential characteristic of these trance states is the sense of oneness between the skier and the mountain.

In contrast, there are many skiers who generate negative trance states through fear or intense self-criticism. When frightened, some imagine "wiping out," frequently talking to themselves about "blowing out their knees."

Others relive past injuries, their stomachs grinding with nausea long before they go down the hill. Some carry on an internal debate whether they should go down or not, seemingly waiting forever before they push over the lip of the hill. There are those whose vision gets cloudy and can't see a line down the hill. All in all, confidence has been eroded and their minds are brain-locked. As a consequence, they usually ski poorly.

Then there are those who denigrate themselves with loud, internal criticism. They call themselves stupid for making silly errors or for not skiing perfectly. Little do they realize how much self-criticism inhibits the exquisite work of the unconscious mind as it controls balance and speed. Nor do they realize that superb skiing is the result of their unconscious mind correcting ongoing, minute errors in their performance.

There's No Such Thing as Perfection in Skiing

It's important to realize that you will never, ever be able to reproduce a run exactly because of the infinite variations of terrain, weather, snow conditions, and your own physiological state. All of this means that there is no such thing as perfection in skiing. In effect, great skiers, like all superb athletes, are masters of correcting their errors.

How does this work? The unconscious mind constantly compares what is actually happening as you ski with mental criterion representations of how you skied really well in the past. When there is a mismatch between these two—what you're actually doing and what you want to do —the unconscious mind automatically makes a correction, with the speed of lightning, to keep you moving as closely matched to your criterion model as possible.

Time and the Unconscious Mind

I'm sure you've experienced being out of control on the mountain one instant and then back in control the next, without knowing how this happened. The paradoxical nature of skiing is to deliberately give way to gravity and then regain your balance and control. In other words, you are constantly on the edge of being out of control. You're moving much too fast to tell yourself consciously exactly how to maintain control.

The conscious mind operates much too slowly to regulate the internal comparison process. It operates linearly— first one thing, then another, and another, in sequence. However, the unconscious mind processes huge amounts of information simultaneously. We know this from reports of many different kinds of athletes, including skiers, who experience dramatic time distortion when skiing superbly in a trance state. They consistently report that time slows down enormously. They are astounded by how slowly they seem to be moving down the hill, when in actuality they are slamming through slalom gates and sailing over knolls at breakneck speeds.

Of course, time doesn't slow down. It proceeds in its usual way, second by second. The illusion of slowness is generated by the fact that the *entranced* skier's quiet and inactive, conscious mind passively observes the pure and unbelievably exquisite and rapid work done by the unconscious mind as it regulates the skier's behavior. When compared to normal, linear, conscious processing, simultaneous, unconscious processing seems like a whirlwind.

Indeed it is. In a flash, the unconscious mind absorbs and integrates all the minute yet critically important cues in the environment that affect performance—icy patches, ruts, moguls, and changes in pitch. Then it automatically corrects muscle tension and body coordination to match the balance and control of a desired performance.

All of this suggests that if superb performance on the hill is the desired outcome, then skiers need to learn how to perform without conscious attention so that the unconscious mind can do its job without interruption. Learning how to perform in a trance state is a marvelous way to learn this.

Many of the metaskills techniques in this book generate mild trance states. Now I want you to learn how to induce profound trance states in yourself so you can learn how to ski even better. But *I caution you* to ski initially only on very gradual, beginners' slopes when in a self-developed trance state. Eventually you may be able to ski difficult terrain in a deliberately induced trance.

The Nature of Trance

Many people have a mistaken notion about trance, believing it's a mystical phenomenon attainable only by some people. It's not. Contrary to the opinion of some hypnosis specialists, *anyone* can learn how to get into a trance. Those who assert that some people cannot be hypnotized are mistaken. The late Dr. Milton H. Erickson, a renowned medical hypnotherapist whose work served as one foundation stone of Neuro-Linguistic Programming, was one of the first to recognize the naturalness of trance, and he incorporated it into his remarkably unique and successful practice.

All people can induce a trance state in themselves—that is, they can change their state of consciousness willfully. It's just a matter of taking time to redevelop the appropriate mental processes to do so. Unfortunately, overemphasis on rationality by our educational system, I believe, has dampened our respect for the role of the unconscious mind in learning and performing.

Children naturally become deeply engrossed in the simple pleasures of watching hawks or kites soar in the sky, of listening to buzzing bees as they hover over flowers to extract their nectar, of feeling the cozy warmth of the sun, of losing track of time and space in front of the television screen. They become transported from the here and now into their own world of fantasy and right-brain mental activity. Their natural capacity to mimic athletes unconsciously is reflected in their almost identical imitations of Doc Gooden or Roger Clemens on the recreational ball fields of America.

Adults, too, know what it's like to alter their states of consciousness, but frequently they forget they know. Like children, they're awed by sunsets, transformed by music, enchanted by novels and stories, absorbed in thought while waiting for a traffic light to change; and their moods are altered by hundreds of everyday experiences in seconds. Trances are induced by riding in elevators, driving long distances on interstate highways, listening to the clickety-clack of the wheels on railroad tracks, making love, focusing intensely on carving a sweeping turn in powder, and recalling the details of a superb skiing maneuver as if they were Sherlock Holmes.

Putting Hypnosis to Work

Having studied and experimented with hypnosis in athletics, I'm convinced that it's perhaps the most powerful tool athletes can use to learn new skills and to maintain consistency in their performance. Essentially, hypnosis is a process of creating, intensifying, and stabilizing an inner state of being with little *conscious* awareness of the environment. Yet, at the same time, the mind knows what is going on externally. Most of my metaskills techniques are based on this process and are designed to tap the resources of the unconscious mind by distracting and quieting the conscious mind.

The Sherlock Holmes Exercise in Chapter Two induces and stabilizes the hypnotic phenomenon of age regression —going back to a former time and place in your life. The M & M Process, colored anchors, and various forms of imagery that were presented in preceding chapters also stimulate hypnotic processes. Metaphors in particular, like storytelling, generate states most conducive to fine athletic performance. Metaskills techniques activate the nondominant hemisphere of the brain, precisely the part of the brain that is fully activated during a trance. These trance states open the door to our world of inner experiences essential to making changes in outward behavior. In essence they free the skier's imagination while skiing.

Several athletes with whom I have worked have experimented with performing *simple, safe skills* after hypnotizing themselves. They invariably report that their performance becomes almost effortless. Figure skaters have traced figures in competition while in a trance; a golfer has developed a way to play golf while deliberately going into a trance just before hitting each shot, returning to a normal state between shots; and a distance swimmer "goes off" into his own world of music while swimming four-hundred-meter and fifteen-hundred-meter races.

Self-Hypnosis

For you to hypnotize yourself requires a certain mind-set to begin with. Essentially, let yourself go and give yourself permission to experience your inner world fully, gradually becoming less and less aware of external reality, like Zen meditation. Let your mind go in a consciously suggested direction, yet allow it to generate whatever sensory representations it wants to with *absolutely no conscious control.* This means letting go of ordinary ways of thinking, adopting an attitude of curiosity, and intensely wanting to learn from the hypnotic experience.

I have taught hundreds of athletes a simple form of self-hypnosis. *Once learned,* you can use it to tap internal resources and achieve important outcomes. The technique was developed by Betty Erickson, Dr. Milton Erickson's wife. I have modified it slightly. It's really quite simple.

Read the following instructions and the descriptions of the reactions of people who have experienced the technique. This will answer some of your questions about what to expect from being in an altered state. Later, when you feel comfortable about hypnotizing yourself, memorize the steps in the process, follow them, and go into an altered state.

The Betty Erickson Technique (Modified)

Sit comfortably in a quiet place where you won't be disturbed. Separate your legs slightly, with your forearms and hands resting comfortably on your thighs. Support your head by resting it against the back of an easy chair or against a wall.

Step 1. Meta Picture

With your eyes open or closed, make a meta picture of yourself seated as you are. When you have a clear meta picture of yourself, gently close your eyes and hold that picture for a few seconds.

Step 2. See, Hear, and Feel

Now, *with your eyes closed, see* pictures in your mind of any *three* objects in the room; *hear* any *three* sounds in the surrounding environment, such as a ticking clock or traffic noises outside; and *feel* any *three* things on the surface of your body. Then see any *two* things, hear any *two* sounds, and feel any *two* physical sensations as before. And then see *one* thing, hear *one* thing, and feel *one* thing.

Step 3. Go to a Place of Pleasure

Now become aware of one hand and arm getting heavier than the other. You can press that hand down against your thigh. I don't know if the lighter arm will begin to bend and your hand will lift upward. If so, the movement will be ever so slow, jerky and automatic. In your mind, go to a place of pleasure, a place where you've been before, where you have thoroughly enjoyed yourself and felt safe and secure. See, hear, and feel again what you saw, heard, and felt before in that special place of yours. Enjoy again the experiences you had there.

At some time during this recollection of pleasure you might begin to notice that the rate and depth of your breathing, your heart rate, and your sense of the weight of your arms and legs have changed. You might also notice that one of your hands has lifted. When you notice any of these changes, use it as a signal to let your mind go wherever it wants to, becoming passively curious about what will happen next in your mind.

Step 4. Back to "Normal"

At some point your unconscious mind will give you a signal —in the form of a personally meaningful image, sound, or bodily sensation—that implies it is time to begin to return to your original, normal state. For instance, if your hand rose during the process, its slow movement downward is a signal to return to normal. Or perhaps you'll see a red light flashing on your mental screen.

Arouse yourself gradually by opening your eyes, looking at the objects around you, listening to the sounds in the environment, and moving parts of your body. Be sure you are fully alert before you engage in an activity that could result in injury.

Reactions to Self-Hypnosis

I've taught the Betty Erickson Technique to many groups of athletes. The following is an account of the reactions of one group immediately after its members had experienced an altered state. At the end of the session the group gradually returned to the here and now. It took about two or three minutes for all to reorient themselves. However, I have known some people to take as long as forty-five minutes to return to what they would call "normal."

"I'm curious to know what reactions, questions, and comments you have about your hypnotic experience," I asked the group when they all appeared to be alert.

Kathryn initiated the response by saying, "I felt as if I'd been asleep, but I know I was listening to your voice and following your suggestions."

It was different for Bruce: "Once my arm started to lift, I just tuned you out altogether. I was in my own world."

In contrast, Maria said, "I was so surprised when my arm started to lift. In the beginning I kept peeking at it, wondering if there was something wrong with me, because it didn't go up. I finally decided to ignore it, and then it started up all by itself."

"I was really disappointed when my arm didn't come up," Gordon commented. "When you said that I didn't have to listen to your voice, I noticed that I got very warm and my arms and legs felt very heavy. It was a pleasant, relaxed feeling. That was certainly a different state from when I started the exercise."

Peter reported his experience by saying, "I sure was surprised when I didn't experience the deep relaxation that I've heard should happen during hypnosis. Instead I felt quite excited."

"My guess," I told him, "is that you were reexperiencing an exciting event in that special place of pleasure."

"That's right," he agreed. "I was riding a huge wave in the surf at the seashore."

Then I asked if any of them had *not* gone into an altered state.

"I didn't," Cheryl answered. "I tried to get relaxed, but it just didn't work."

"That's okay," I said. "This technique might not be the best way for you. Or perhaps you didn't follow the instructions. You said that you *'tried* to relax.' That's a difficult thing to do. Trying to relax is like trying to be spontaneous or trying to go to sleep. Those three states—relaxation, spontaneity, and sleep—just happen; they can't be engineered."

If you have an experience similar to Cheryl's, I suggest you do the exercise several more times. If you're still unsuccessful, it doesn't mean you are unhypnotizable. It merely means that another form of hypnosis, tailored to your individual way of processing sensory information, is necessary. Deciding the most useful form, however, requires some individual attention by a qualified clinician.

Some people fear a loss of control under hypnosis. To learn this technique requires that you give up a certain amount of control by your conscious mind and let yourself go, the way I want you to ski a familiar trail—mindlessly. It's important to trust the process and allow your unconscious mind to take care of you as it has throughout your life.

Whether you realize it or not, your unconscious mind has been taking care of you all along. For example, with your conscious mind you make a decision to turn at a particular place on the hill. As you're turning, your unconscious mind controls and coordinates all the muscles in your legs as you steer; things are going too fast for your conscious mind to tell individual muscles when to contract and release. Take tying your shoes as another example. You learn to tie them consciously, and now you probably tie them unconsciously, without thinking.

Having said this, I recognize that it is very important to be wary of someone else hypnotizing you. Hypnosis can be used manipulatively, especially if you're overly susceptible to the suggestions and influence of other people. However, I'm teaching a process that you'll use by yourself. Therefore, it requires that you have trust in yourself. When you have this trust, you'll be able to tap the power of your unconscious mind and make changes in your behavior while in an altered state.

The last question in the group session came from Loren. She asked, "Can you get stuck in an altered state and not be aware of danger, a fire, or an intruder?"

"My personal experience with self-hypnosis," I replied, "and the reported experiences of hundreds of others with whom I've worked, is that the unconscious mind is constantly and protectively monitoring the environment while you're in an altered state. When something very unusual occurs, you will be aroused from the trance state. As for getting stuck, I don't know anyone who stayed hypnotized longer than the time they set aside for it. It's possible, however, that you could fall asleep if your body needs rest. When that happens, the hypnotic state is erased."

Experiencing Self-Hypnosis

If, after reading about the reactions to the Betty Erickson Technique, you feel comfortable and can see yourself doing it, go back to page 142 and reread the steps in the process. Memorize them and go to a quiet place where you won't be disturbed while experiencing the technique.

I encourage you to practice it every few days for several weeks until you can put yourself into an altered state within a couple of minutes. Each time you use it, decide on the amount of time you want to remain in an altered state so you can return to your normal activities when you want to. Your unconscious mind has its own timer, and I think you'll be surprised to discover that you'll "come back" within a minute or two of the time you have allotted for yourself.

It's important to monitor carefully your state of consciousness *after* you return to the here and now. Determine exactly how long it takes you to return completely to your normal state of functioning. Most people return to a "normal" state in moments; a few take up to an hour. It's possible to injure yourself if you engage in a potentially harmful activity before you're back to your normal state.

Applying Self-Hypnosis

Self hypnosis can be used in many ways to achieve worthwhile outcomes pertaining directly to skiing as well as to your general well-being. For the purposes of this book, I'll concentrate on the application of self-hypnosis to improved skiing performance.

Improving Athletic Skills

I once worked with a high jumper who wasn't jumping as well as he had been. He experimented with modifying several parts of his performance, but without success. He decided to try self-hypnosis, instructing his unconscious mind to attend to the task of improving his jumping. During one session he had an image of a space shuttle blasting off from Cape Canaveral. He interpreted this image to mean that he should apply more energy during his takeoff.

It seemed obvious, yet he hadn't thought of it during his experiments. So at his next practice session he created the metaphorical image of a space shuttle at the time of take-off, and he soared over the bar with an inch or two to spare.

There are several ways to improve your skiing through self-hypnosis. One is to give yourself the suggestion beforehand to experience fully a particular problem you are having with a certain kind of skiing maneuver, followed by an experience that is exactly the opposite—when you were skiing well. Then put yourself into an altered state and learn how to correct your performance from the images that are unconsciously produced. After "coming back" from the altered state, compare the images of good and bad skiing, looking for ways to correct your movements. This is similar to using Discovering Difference and the Get-It-Back Process.

Videotapes and Self-Hypnosis

Another way to use self-hypnosis involves watching continuous loops of videotape recordings of professional skiers just before and just *after* you've put yourself into an altered state. Here is how Jerry Beilinson, an advanced skier, and I worked with a videotape of several highly skilled skiers. We integrated the Get-It Process with self-hypnosis. We worked together both on and off the snow, and the result was considerable improvement in Jerry's short-radius turns.

Working off the Snow

A week before he went on a skiing trip to Utah and Tahoe, Jerry daily observed a short segment of a video in which two skiers demonstrated short-radius turns. First he watched the video without paying attention to anything special. Then he watched the video again, pretending he was in the body of one of the demonstrators but wearing his own skiing gear. While watching, he paid careful attention to how his muscles felt while he was mentally skiing. After that, he watched the video a third time, again just to watch. The purpose of these observation exercises was to train Jerry to watch without conscious judgment and to help him learn how to run his brain in a special way.

After he had watched the video for about ten minutes, Jerry shut off the VCR and reproduced, in his mind, images of one of the model demonstrators skiing. Then he created meta pictures of himself skiing as if he were the model. Finally he imagined, using regular pictures, that he was actually skiing on a slope, feeling the balance and control necessary to ski like his model. All of this was done in a "normal" state. The purpose of this sequence of mental activity was to prepare Jerry to do it all easily while in a trance.

Just before putting himself into an altered state, Jerry instructed his unconscious mind by saying, "While watching the video, focus on the salient features of the demonstrator's performance that are most important to improve my skiing." By instructing his unconscious mind this way, it relieved his conscious mind from having to watch. In that way he could just be curious about whatever his unconscious mind might eventually uncover.

While in a trance, Jerry watched the video without paying attention to anything in particular. After returning to a normal state, he made notes of what his unconscious mind uncovered. In particular he noted that even in a short-radius turn his model's approach to it was exceptionally long and unhurried. This allowed him gradually to increase sustained pressure of his edges against the snow before a powerful release into the next turn—a fundamental element of good skiing.

Jerry also noted a relaxed and "centeredness" of the model's upper body. He said the model skier ". . . was skiing as if floating, without tilting from side to side and without bobbing up and down." Finally, Jerry noticed how the model held his hands out front, making distinct pole plants just as each turn began.

On the Mountain

Jerry's report of his Utah and Tahoe ski experiences was one of both pleasant surprise and disappointment. "My first run and the first sections of the next couple of runs," Jerry reported, "were good—about a '7+.' I was pleased and surprised, thinking, 'Gee, this works. It's what I had imagined would happen.' It was different from my usual skiing. I was making clean, round, short-radius turns. Usually I ski bigger turns. My feet and legs were winding and unwinding in a steady way, and I was relaxed without my upper body being involved."

As for Jerry's disappointment, he said that the quality of the first few runs didn't persist. He couldn't reproduce his performance time after time. This may have resulted from the fact that he did not get his good performances properly anchored. Although he said he created several metaphorical anchors, none of them worked. To offset his disappointment, I told him that I would work further with him when we got on the mountain together.

Before Jerry left for his trip, I had instructed him to watch the video in an altered state early in the morning before skiing. However, he didn't have access to a VCR. Nonetheless, he induced an altered state and pretended that he was watching himself ski in the body of his model.

While riding the chair lift, Jerry consciously rehearsed skiing as if he were the model, using regular movies. Finally, just before shoving off, he created an internal meta movie of himself skiing well. This movie was superimposed on the section of the trail immediately in front of him.

Working on Snow Together

Shortly after returning from his western ski trip, Jerry and I spent about four hours together at Hunter Mountain, New York. Initially I had let Jerry use his own form of meditation to get himself into an altered state. Since it appeared that he wasn't in a very deep trance, I decided to teach him the Betty Erickson Technique. At Hunter I had him do it several times; each time he went into deeper and more relaxed states. While he was in an altered state, I told his unconscious mind to watch his model skier in his mind's eye, and become aware of whatever mechanics were important for him to ski short-radius turns better.

Self-hypnosis worked, although it took about four or five runs before Jerry was able to feel sustained improvement in his turns. Finally something clicked. It was a slingshot feeling that Jerry felt when he released as he came out of his turns. Although he liked this new feeling, at times he lost control. The amounts of force and speed generated by the slingshot action were sometimes unmanageable. Knowing that when Jerry skied well he felt power and control stemming from his gut, I suggested he think about absorbing the power in his gut so he could more easily control it. This worked.

At the end of the next run he said, "I had lots of good, short turns, with power and control. It was as if I had a power spring between my gut and my skis. I directed the power from the mountain to my gut when I released at the end of one turn, and then I sent power back to my feet to create pressure on the mountain as I moved into the next turn."

At the end of the day, Jerry asked me how he could make his high level of performance stick. I told him to imagine a spring and associate it with feelings of controlled power moving back and forth between his skis and his gut. At the same time, he was to associate this image with adjusting his pole straps (a K-anchor) just before he started down the hill. I told him to practice this four or five times each day, on and off the snow, until the image of the spring and the slingshot feelings were generated automatically whenever he adjusted his pole straps. I suggested that he could literally adjust his pole straps at home while seated in an armchair. He wasn't used to holding ski poles in an armchair, but he agreed nonetheless.

Although Jerry says the jury is still out on whether he can consistently ski with the same feelings of controlled power, he admits that he has learned some important things. "I have a new way of turning that feels right," he said, "and I have a surefire way to get into an altered state. I've also learned some things about how my brain works."

It is clear to me that Jerry has learned one of the most important fundamentals of Downhill skiing—the slingshot feeling. And he did it on his own, with a little mind consultation from me, using videotape and self-hypnosis.

Some ski shops have videotapes of fine skiers for sale or rent at reasonable rates. It's also possible to tape skiers shown on TV broadcasts. These tapes can be made into continuous video loops. The cost varies from one area of the country to another, but it can be done in a week's time for less than fifty dollars.

Here are the steps to follow if you want to combine self-hypnosis with video observation. The fundamental idea is to refine and groove your skiing maneuvers in your mind and muscles by watching an outstanding skier on videotape while in an altered state, and then mimic him on the mountain.

VIDEO MIMICRY

In an armchair:

1. Select or make your own videotape of a top skier making repeated turns that you want to mimic. Watch the video without judgment; just watch. If there's sound, turn it off.

2. Watch the video again, but this time pretend to see yourself skiing (meta pictures) in place of the model skier, and feel the muscle action required.

3. Without the video, imagine skiing down a familiar trail while reproducing the movements of the model skier. Use regular pictures.

4. Tell your unconscious mind to pay attention to the parts of the model's skiing that will make your skiing better. Put yourself into an altered state and repeat Step 2.

5. When finished watching your model skier, allow yourself to come back to your "normal" state, and make notes of the important elements of the model's performance identified by your unconscious mind.

6. Repeat Step 3, reproducing the elements identified in Step 5.

7. Repeat Steps 1 through 6 once a day for about a week before going skiing.

On the mountain:

1. Before breakfast, put yourself into an altered state. Using regular pictures, imagine yourself skiing down a familiar trail executing the important elements identified in Step 5 above.

2. On the lift, imagine skiing down a familiar trail executing the important elements identified in Step 5 above. Use regular pictures.

3. At the top of an *easy* run, see yourself skiing well in your mind (a meta movie). Superimpose this meta movie on the trail in front of you. Clear your mind, push off, and ski with minimum or no thought. Just ski.

4. Using the Get-It Process (see page 129), make corrections in your performance until you're satisfied with the degree to which you have mimicked your model skier's performance.

5. Anchor the feelings of your performance to a natural and necessary movement you make before pushing off the lip of the hill (Jerry used the adjustment of his pole straps for his anchor).

6. Practice firing the anchor on and off the snow until it becomes automatic.

7. Select a more difficult run. Visualize your line, and chart your course down the hill. Fire the anchor to get yourself into the just-right state, and then ski with little or no conscious thought.

Be patient with yourself as you experiment with self-hypnosis. Give yourself time to become adept at it by practicing regularly. Once learned, it can be used to accomplish all sorts of desired outcomes.

NINE

Mind and Body: Controlling Pain and Hastening Healing

Although most skiers remain healthy and in one piece, some have serious injuries, especially when racing. Part of the attraction of skiing is the lure of speed and the challenge to overcome danger. When misfortune strikes and accidents occur, skiers are faced with the tasks of managing pain, tolerating extensive periods of healing, and then overcoming the doubt and fear of getting back on skis again.

The mind, exquisitely adept at controlling movement, is equally effective at altering the perception of pain and facilitating the body's natural healing capacities. This chapter describes several techniques that can help you get back on the mountain as quickly as possible after you've been injured.

These techniques are based on the principle that the mind affects the internal working of all the organs and systems of the body. Although we have very little hard scientific evidence to verify this principle, many physicians and other health specialists support it.

I know from my clinical experience, as do other medical and mental health specialists, that the mind acts like a powerful anesthetic. It heals without chemical supplements or scalpels, and it supplements medication and the work of surgeons. Evidence that the mind is a pain reducer is reflected in the experience of those who undergo chest and abdominal surgery with self-hypnosis and *without* anesthesia. The mind's healing power is also manifested through the work of faith healers, shamans, and Native American medicine men. Mental healing has been demonstrated by hundreds of people who have cured themselves of all sorts of diseases.

If you're genuinely skeptical about these assertions, all I ask is that you experience doing the techniques. Find out what happens when you use them. The absolute worst that can happen, if they work, is that you'll no longer have pain and injury as excuses. But before using them, I encourage you to consult your physician if you are emotionally upset or have unexplained pain or physical symptoms. My techniques are meant to complement the work of health specialists, not replace their services.

Pain Control

When pain is present, the appropriate action is to consult medical specialists to identify its cause and provide appropriate treatment and medication. If, however, pain persists, you can learn how to reduce it while still undergoing medical treatment. Let's consider two pain-reducing techniques.

Inside Out

Inside Out is a technique that effectively reduces pain, especially resulting from emotional stress, such as headaches. I've used it with hundreds of people. It's a very simple six-step process, as illustrated by the work below I did with Gail, who complained of having a severe headache with no apparent cause.

"On a scale from 0 to 10," I said, "rate the severity of the pain you're experiencing right now."

"It's a doozy," she replied. "Ten!"

"What I want you to do," I instructed her, "is imagine what that pain looks like. Describe it to me as if you were looking at it on the wall over there. In fact, project the image of your pain on the wall and tell me precisely what it looks like."

"What it looks like?" she asked, looking puzzled.

"Sure. Tell me its shape and how big it is."

Gail paused, stared at the wall, and then said, "It's shaped like a small football. It's expanding and contracting, as if it were being squeezed. That's the way it feels here in the back of my head."

"Fine description," I said. "Tell me about its color, texture, and density."

"It's glowing red. It's really heavy and seems to be filled with thick pieces of rubber. It's very smooth, like plastic."

"Can you see that smooth, pulsating, glowing, red football filled with rubber on the wall right now?"

Gail nodded as her eyes focused on the wall.

"Hold that image there while doing something that may sound strange to you," I said. "Make a sound, either out loud or privately to yourself, that exactly matches the way your headache feels. Open your throat and let that feeling of pain come out."

Gail's eyes became unfocused as she uttered a rather feeble "Ow."

"Open your throat, Gail, and let that sound come out freely and strongly," I told her.

This time Gail wailed loudly. "Oooowwww!"

"That's right. Keep your throat open and adjust the sound so that it matches your pain."

After listening to her wail for about ten seconds I interrupted her: "Stop the sound for a few seconds. In your peripheral vision, project another image on the wall, an image of a place of pleasure where you've been in the past. Put that picture on the left edge of your vision and keep the football image of your pain in the center."

"Okay, I've got the two pictures," she said.

I told her to start making the sound that matched her pain again and to keep it going. Then I instructed her to imagine a wind blowing from left to right across her pictures.

"Let the image of the pain vaporize and be blown away by the wind," I said, "as the picture of your place of pleasure moves to the center of your vision."

After about a minute Gail seemed to relax. Her posture slumped as her mouth opened and her chin dropped. I asked her, "On a scale of 0 to 10, what's the intensity of your pain now?"

She paused for a few seconds and then said, "Two. The headache's almost gone. That's amazing. Can I use that process for other headaches and other pains?"

I told her it can be used for any kind of pain anytime, but she should check out her headaches and other persistent pains with her doctor.

INSIDE OUT

1. Identify the precise location of your pain and rate its severity on a scale from 0 to 10.

2. Project a clear image of the pain on a nearby surface. Identify its size, shape, density, weight, thickness, surface texture, and color.

3. Holding that image in view, make a sound that matches its intensity. The sound should express exactly how the pain feels. If it's inconvenient to utter the sound aloud, "hear" it loud and clear in your mind. Vary its pitch, tone, and volume until it matches the feeling and intensity of your pain.

4. In your peripheral vision to the left, project an image of a remembered place of pleasure.

5. Again focus on the projected image of pain, express what it feels like—vocally or silently—and pretend that the pain image is vaporizing. As it disappears, gradually lower the sound and let the image of the place of pleasure move to the center of your vision.

6. Rate the severity of pain that remains on a scale from 0 to 10. Compare it with the original rating in Step 1.

The Inside Out technique usually reduces a painful headache considerably or eliminates it altogether. Metaphorically, you move the pain from inside your body to the outside; thus the title "Inside Out." The technique can be

used for other forms of pain, especially at a time immediately following an injury.

Self-Hypnosis

Accidents in skiing frequently result in multiple, painful
bruises that can't be soothed by the Inside Out process.
However, pain can be reduced through self-hypnosis. I
learned a process of alleviating multiple sources of pain
with self-hypnosis from a twelve-year-old girl who suffered
from sickle-cell anemia.

Her technique is as follows:

Imagine a console of dials on your mental screen. Each
dial needle indicates the intensity of a particular pain you
may have in a specific part of your body. Each dial has a
control knob used to regulate the intensity of the pain. If
you turn the knob in one direction, the needle moves to the
right and the pain increases; if you turn it in the opposite
direction, the needle moves to the left and the pain subsides.

While you're in an altered state, see an imaginary strand
of nerves that connects each painful area of your body to a
separate dial on your mental console. At the same time
make an internal sound the way each pain actually feels at
that moment. The more intense the pain, the louder the
sound.

To reduce the pain, first increase—yes, increase—the
intensity of one particular pain by turning the knob under
the proper dial in one direction. As the needle registers a
higher intensity of pain, feel the pain increase and hear the
sound become louder. Then turn the knob in the opposite
direction to reduce the pain and volume of sound as much
as possible.

Repeat this procedure for each separate pain. Bring yourself back from the altered state to "normal." The pain or pains should be eliminated entirely or reduced at least to a tolerable level.

Emotional Distress

Many times skiers repeatedly suffer mental anguish when they recall a serious skiing accident and think about the effects of it on their lives. They sometimes berate themselves for supposedly being careless, or they become depressed thinking their skiing days might be over. Two examples of people who suffered emotional distress after a skiing accident come to mind. In both cases, the skiers generated an entirely different perspective of their accidents after reliving the traumatic incident.

Trauma Reduction

Jessica Zufolo seriously injured her left knee several years ago while skiing out of bounds at Steamboat Springs, Colorado. She came to me recently saying that her accident left her feeling reluctant to ski again. She wanted to prove to herself that she could overcome the mental obstacles that stood in her way of getting back on skis.

Fear of reinjuring her knee was a big deterrent to her willingness to get back on skis. This fear was compounded by feelings of guilt for having skied out of bounds. To top it off, she believed she was a failure because she had not been able to master skiing as she had done with gymnastics and other sports. All in all, she felt ambivalent about skiing again, somewhat driven to overcome her fear, but lacking self-confidence.

To help Jessica get a different perspective, I told her that I was going to have her reexperience her skiing accident from a distance. My hope was that she could return to skiing after we had finished.

"First of all," I said, "I want you to remember a specific experience in your life, not necessarily a skiing experience, when you were operating confidently and effectively performing up to your own standard of excellence. As you think about this, I want you to anchor the feelings of that state of confident effectiveness by squeezing my wrist. Correlate the strength of the squeeze with the intensity of the feeling. When the feeling gets stronger, squeeze harder; when it subsides, reduce the intensity of the squeeze. Do you understand?"

"Hmm-hmm."

"Good. In your mind, go back to that confident and effective experience and see, hear, and feel again what you saw, heard, and felt then. As the feeling develops, just squeeze my wrist. Deliberately let the feeling subside, increase, and subside again so you know you're in control of it."

After she had accessed and anchored her resourceful state, I asked, "What are the physical sensations associated with that state?"

"I feel strong in my arms and legs, and my chest feels like it's a full ball of fire."

"Now I want you to relive your skiing accident in a very special way. But before you start to relive it, make an internal picture of yourself seated here as if you are behind yourself; this is what I call the 'meta position.' Now see yourself looking at an imaginary screen in front of you. It's as if you were in a movie projection booth looking down on yourself seated in a theater and looking at a movie screen. Can you do that?"

After about ten to fifteen seconds Jessica said she could. Then I told her to put *only the first frame* of a movie of her skiing accident and its aftermath on the imaginary screen in front of her. I also instructed her to grab my wrist so she could fire the anchor of confident effectiveness at any time during her accident movie. If she felt weak or frightened, all she had to do was squeeze my wrist to access that powerful resource. The squeeze also provided me with feedback information about the degree to which she felt anxious while she relived the accident.

"We're ready to begin," I said. "Float out into the meta position behind yourself and see us here now, today, looking at your younger self in the first frame of your accident movie. Got it?"

"Hmm-hmm."

"Good. Let the movie of the accident roll, making sure you stay in the meta position. Fire your resource anchor whenever needed to make the viewing of the movie free of pain and anxiety. As you watch the movie, study it carefully and notice what actually happened, starting with the accident and extending through the treatment and healing of your knee. You're on a learning expedition to find out how your younger self dealt with that entire situation.

"Discover what you did then that you hadn't realized you had done. Notice that you did all that you knew how to do. Find something about the experience you didn't know you knew—about how effective you were even though you were hurt. Run the movie several times, if necessary, until you're satisfied that you have learned all that's possible from it."

When Jessica finished, I had her float back into herself and watch the movie directly once more, wondering to herself if she could learn even more.

When she had finished her second review, I said, "Now, see your younger self on the screen and hold both of your hands out in front of you. Pretend you are reaching into that screen. Take hold of younger Jessica and bring her into your arms. Hold and comfort her, telling her silently what she needed to hear then that no one told her. Tell her you're from her future and will take care of her from now on.

"As you're comforting her, feel her come into your body. Let the feeling of her energy spread to your head, neck, chest, back, arms, hips, legs."

As I noticed Jessica's skin color change and her breathing deepen, I said, "Now use her energy and your new knowledge to gain a different perspective of several other past experiences, nodding when you've finished that."

When I saw her nod, I instructed her to turn around, in her mind, and face her future. I told her to apply the knowledge gained from reviewing her accident to pending experiences that seemed fearful or puzzling. Finally I said, "Comfort and praise yourself now as someone who has learned a great deal about yourself that could be useful for understanding other parts of your past as well as the experiences yet to come.

"I don't know if you should ski again, but you can allow your unconscious mind to work in its own way and at its own speed to inform you in a special, clear, and unambiguous way that you are, or are not, ready to ski again. . . . And when you sense you have done enough, come back to the here and now."

After she opened her eyes and became accustomed to

the light, I asked Jessica how she felt. "I feel cleansed in a way, as if I've resolved my negative feelings toward the accident. I also realize that the accident is an example of how I was living my life at the time. I was naive, impatient, and unrealistic about being the best at everything I did—all of which helped to cause my accident. Now I don't *have* to get back on the mountain. I'm still not sure what to do about skiing again, but it's okay for me to be unsure. Before, I hated my ambivalence; now I'm purged of it."

After a short period of discussion, I asked Jessica to call me in a month or two to let me know what she had decided to do about skiing. When we subsequently spoke, she said the work we had done had affected her significantly. Specifically, she said, "I have more control over my life than I had realized. I've learned how to trust myself, to take more responsibility for my health, and to stop my frenetic lifestyle."

As for skiing again she said, "If the opportunity arises to go skiing, then I'll probably go."

"What happened to your fear of skiing again?"

"I really don't have any," she asserted.

Even though Jessica doesn't fully understand what happened during the trauma-reduction process, it is clear that she achieved several substantial outcomes: she lost her fear of skiing; she reframed the meaning of her accident into something positive; she gained considerable insight into herself, recognizing that she had more control of her life than she had realized; and she increased her self-confidence.

The following is a step-by-step description of the process I used with Jessica. You, too, can use it to reframe almost any kind of traumatic event of your own so it becomes a positive learning experience instead of remaining a source of anxiety and anguish.

TRAUMA REDUCTION

1. Remember an experience when you were at your very best, being confidently effective. Anchor the resource of effectiveness by squeezing your fist.

2. In front of you, create an imaginary screen on which you will later run a complete movie of a past skiing accident, the treatment of your injuries, and your recovery.

3. In your mind, put yourself into the "meta position," looking at yourself watching the imaginary screen. Pretend you're in a movie projection booth looking at yourself seated in a theater and watching a movie.

4. Remaining in the meta position, run the movie of your skiing accident several times; fire your resource anchor (squeeze your fist) whenever you experience pain or anxiety while watching the movie.

5. Study the movie thoroughly to identify what actually happened, recognizing that you did all that could have been expected of you at the time.

6. Study the movie again, but this time look at it *directly*, not from the meta position.

7. See yourself on the screen at the end of the experience. Tell your younger self what he or she would have wanted to hear at the time of the accident but didn't.

8. Literally extend your arms and pretend to bring your younger self into your arms. Feel the energy of your younger self and let that feeling spread throughout your body.

9. Comfort your younger self by saying whatever else needs to be said.

10. Reflect on what you have learned.

Reframing

The Canadian World Cup skier Liisa Savijarvi had a more serious accident while preparing for the last World Cup Downhill of the 1987 season at Vail, Colorado, eleven months before the '88 Olympics. Although I didn't work with Liisa to reframe her mental perspective of skiing, her experiences are instructive. Without knowing it she was using some NLP and metaskills techniques. I'll describe what she did, and then summarize them in the form of a special technique you can use.

At the time of her accident, the light on the racecourse was "flat," making it impossible for her to see the crests of bumps and landing areas clearly. Had pine boughs been placed on the course below each bump, she could have at least seen the landing areas. Consequently, when she suddenly came upon a crest, she took off unprepared and landed straight-legged instead of flexed. The jar of her landing shattered a couple of vertebrae, and the fall "trashed" her leg.

Liisa said the accident left her feeling devastated. "I had an overall feeling of no confidence. In an instant my life was changed. I went from having a focus to not knowing what was ahead. Skiing had been my life since I was four-teen months old. I spent more time on skis than I did off during my competitive career. I raced in '84 at Sarajevo and was looking forward to Calgary." Unfortunately, there was insufficient time for Liisa to rehabilitate herself for the '88 Winter Olympics.

To overcome her feelings, Liisa put herself through an extensive program of mental adjustment. First, she repeat-edly replayed in her mind the details of her skiing acci-dent, just as Jessica did. Liisa realized that she had skied as well as possible under the circumstances. This, she said, helped to restore some of her self-confidence in her skiing ability.

Second, Liisa reframed her disappointment during her extended period of physical therapy when she saw other rehabilitation patients with much more severe and un-remediable disabilities. She said, "I came to the full realiza-tion that I was alive and that I could ski again. I considered myself extremely lucky that I could even walk."

Liisa made a rather dramatic shift in her hard-driving attitude toward achieving high-level goals. Although she remained goal-oriented, she no longer put pressure on herself to achieve as she had done when she was compet-ing internationally. She didn't *have* to rehabilitate herself quickly, nor did she *have* to get back on the mountain right away.

Because her perspective changed so abruptly, I asked her to explain how she took the pressure off herself.

"I think it came about because I didn't want to disappoint myself anymore. It was pretty unrealistic, at that point, to expect to be skiing in the Olympics. That had been my goal for twenty years; not to reach it was pretty disappointing. I thought that if I could just ski again and make a few turns, that would be great, a bonus.

"And maybe the shift in my attitude went back to the luck I had right after the accident. It's a miracle I didn't sever my spinal cord while lifting myself onto the toboggan and moving about in the hospital. I was not only lucky once, I was lucky a hundred times. And now I don't even buy lottery tickets. I figured I used up my luck."

Liisa also believed that her attitude shifted during her physical rehabilitation because she not only realized she had accomplished something few people can achieve—winning a World Cup event—but she found other things to do, in addition to recreational skiing, that gave her pleasure: spending time with her husband, her home, her family, business, dinner with friends, and other simple things.

Liisa decided to get back on skis nine months after her accident. I asked her if she had been afraid, and if so, how she managed her fear when she first skied again. She replied, "I knew I could ski because I had skied for so many years. But I was afraid because I didn't know how my leg would feel. I wondered if it was going to hurt or give out."

It turned out that Liisa had completely rehabilitated her knee and back. She said, "I listened to the doctor for the first time in my life."

Liisa managed her fear in a number of ways. "I spent some time doing mental preparation, feeling like I was standing in my old ski boots and sliding on an old pair of skis. I wanted to get back the same old feelings. I thought about keeping my hands up, getting myself into a balanced position, looking down the hill, and planning my turns." In essence, without knowing it Liisa had become Sherlock Holmes, accessing her resources of having skied superbly in the past.

On the first outing, she went to the flattest hill around with her junior coach, Rob Roy, and some of her current teammates, who provided her with emotional support. She started with the simplest maneuvers: first a snowplow, then a couple of turns. At the time, she said to herself, "I'm going to take one step at a time. I'm going to do what feels good. If my knee feels good, I'll do another turn." Later, she recalled, "My thoughts were so simple in comparison to what I would think about in a starting gate. I didn't expect to be running slalom gates by the end of the day. I put in my mind practical goals—goals that I could easily reach, like just sliding and turning again."

After doing a few turns without pain, Liisa realized that she'd forgotten nothing and could ski again. Pleased with this outcome, she gradually extended her skiing practice, building up to more and more turns, "taking each day one at a time," she said. "If my knee was sore, I'd stop skiing. I'd take a day off."

She summed up her changed attitude toward skiing by asking herself some rhetorical questions: "What if I just go out and ski? What if I pass on information to the younger kids? What if I can help *them* win World Cups?"

At the present time, Liisa skis regularly and runs a ladies' midweek "Ski Escape Program" at Nakiska in Alberta, site of the '88 Winter Olympics. She has capitalized on her experience by teaching her students good mental skills and helping them manage their fears.

Thinking back on the experiences of Jessica and Liisa, it's clear that each of them reframed the meaning of their accidents after mentally playing them over and over again. Jessica saw her accident as a reflection of her personality. Liisa assessed hers as something that couldn't have been prevented, given the weather and snow conditions. Both modified their beliefs and life-values. And most importantly, each regained her self-confidence. By reliving their experiences, by squarely facing their problems, and by accessing their resources, they found ways to change and grow.

Here is a step-by-step procedure you can use to reframe your own skiing accident and get back on the mountain again, feeling confident:

REFRAMING

1. Use the Trauma Reduction technique (see page 168) to get a different perspective of your skiing accident.

2. Thoroughly rebuild your physical strength, relying on a medical opinion that you are sufficiently healed to ski again.

3. Use the Sherlock Holmes Exercise (see page 31) periodically to access your resources of skiing well in the past as a way to prepare yourself to ski again.

4. Rethink the priority of skiing in your life. Determine just how important it is in relation to other life-values and life-beliefs.

5. With professional help and emotional support from others, ski again on as flat a hill as possible.

6. Set simple, realistic skiing goals. If there's no pain while executing basic maneuvers, move *slowly* on to more advanced skills. When soreness develops, stop for a day or two until it subsides.

7. Assess the quality of your skiing and the amount of pleasure you derive from it. Use this assessment to determine how much you will ski in the future.

8. Look to your future and decide what you want to do—that is, pretend you are doing certain things and notice if it feels good doing them. If so, you have a blueprint for your life yet to come.

Healing

During the past eight to ten years many books focusing on the mind-body relationship, especially as it relates to illness and healing, have been written for laypeople. You might find some of them of particular interest: *Anatomy of an Illness* by Norman Cousins; *Getting Well Again* by Carl Simonton, a cancer specialist, and his associates; *Love, Medicine & Miracles* by Bernie Siegel, a surgeon; and *Minding the Body, Mending the Mind* by Joan Borysenko, director of the Mind/Body Clinic at Harvard Medical School. A more technical book that explains the theory behind mental healing is *The Psychobiology of Mind-Body Healing* by Ernest Rossi, a protégé of Dr. Milton Erickson.

Norman Cousins clearly demonstrates the power of his natural healing resources. Together with his doctor's encouragement and medical expertise, and through humorous movies, books, and cartoons, he overcame his depression and disease. Laughter, and the positive emotional state it evoked, proved to be important parts of his cure.

Bernie Siegel and Carl Simonton have demonstrated the power of the mind as an adjunct to medical treatment for cancer patients. Joan Borysenko describes an extensive preventive medicine program of mental techniques to supplement medical treatment at Harvard.

According to respected scientists, we are able to heal ourselves by using mental processes. Simply stated, they believe our thoughts and emotions affect body chemistry, especially hormones and neuropeptides. These chemicals affect our immune system's response to disease.

The essential elements of mental healing are a belief in your own power to heal yourself, and your ability to visualize accurately the physiological healing processes that help the body repair itself with or without the use of medicine and surgery.

Here are some examples of how several of my clients hastened their healing with several metaskills techniques.

Torn Ankle Ligaments

Cynthia, a young figure skater who had orthopedic surgery for a serious foot injury, enhanced her recovery by her own unusual visualization process. She "saw" boatloads of little men in white hospital coats traveling through her bloodstream to the site of the injury. They unloaded special ligament-stretching paraphernalia, sewing machines, and chemical nutriments. They then stretched the ligaments, sewed them securely to the bones in her foot, and sprinkled medicine on top of the ligaments.

She also visualized a crew of garbage collectors who cleaned up the waste left by her interior tailors and by the body's natural healing processes. They loaded the waste onto scows that were dispersed through her blood vessels to her liver, kidneys, intestines, and lungs for eventual disposal outside of her body.

Cynthia held her own matinee movies every day during recovery. When she left the hospital, her doctor told her that she had recovered from the surgery in an amazingly short time.

Knee Surgery

Here's a personal testimony. In the early 1970s I had surgery on my left knee for a torn ligament. Ten years later I had severe pain and limited movement in my right knee. The orthopedic surgeon who had diagnosed my injury and assisted in the left-knee surgery told me the same problem now existed in my right knee. He prescribed surgery identical to the previous procedure.

I told him I wanted to use visualization to heal my knee before I underwent any surgery. I asked him to describe fully what had to happen for my knee to heal naturally. Although he was extremely skeptical, as many orthopedists are, he told me what would have to happen inside the knee capsule. I left his office, and he wished me success.

I created a metaphorical movie to activate the healing process, and watched it daily in my mind for a couple of weeks and then once a week for several months. Within a month I no longer had pain. It is now almost twelve years later, and I still have no pain. I had no surgery, and I'm as active as I was before my right knee acted up. I attribute this to my healing movie.

The following is a description of a simple visualization method of mental healing that I have developed and used successfully with scores of athletes; it doesn't *always* work. The method is based primarily on Carl Simonton's work. You, too, can use it as a supplement to the treatment and medication prescribed by your physician.

METASKILLS HEALING

1. Ask your physician to give you a complete and accurate description, in mechanical and chemical terms, of what must happen in your body to bring it back to normal, including the effects of medication on the healing processes. Make sure you understand exactly what that process is by restating to your doctor in your own words his or her description. When the doctor verifies your layperson's description, it becomes the basis for creating your own mental-healing movie.

2. Create a movie that metaphorically represents the mechanical and chemical processes of healing. (For example, a balloon deflating could represent a reduction in swelling; a weaver working on a loom could signify the rejoining of torn tissue.)

3. "Run" your movie several times a day. Include a segment in the movie that portrays you as gradually healing, regaining energy, and becoming physically active again.

4. After successful healing, praise yourself for the work you've done.

If your condition doesn't improve after a week or so of visualization, the process you've been using may need to be continued for several more weeks, or it may need to be changed. The ineffectiveness of your metaphorical movie could be the result of incomplete medical knowledge, since physicians are not always totally sure of exactly how medications work or precisely how the body heals. Therefore the movie may not represent the recovery process accurately.

Your unconscious mind will indicate where the movie is inaccurate if you see distorted images, hear muffled sounds, or feel uncomfortable as you watch. Corrections, based on more knowledge from your doctor and better interpretation of that knowledge on your part, can be made in the movie wherever you experience distorted sensory information.

If your health status has not improved after changing the movie and watching it for several more weeks, it makes sense to abandon the process, and perhaps see another doctor.

T E N

Après Ski

What you think about skiing, what you want to get from the sport, and how you think while you're actually skiing are equally important. In this chapter I'll present a few ideas about how you can achieve your most desired skiing outcomes and how you can free yourself to enjoy the sport fully. I'll discuss the value of having realistic expectations, point out how you can identify your outcomes, and guide you in the selection of appropriate metaskills techniques to achieve them.

Expectations

Just how realistic are you about your skiing? Upon arrival at the mountain, do you immediately take the lift to the top of the most difficult trail even though you're an intermediate skier? Do you try to impress your friends by attempting to match their far superior skills? Do you succumb to their encouragement to ski a trail far more difficult than you can manage? When I see klutzy skiers creating a yard sale on extremely steep slopes, or see ashen, drawn faces at the crest of a black diamond trail, it looks as though they expect a whole lot more than is possible for skiers of their ability. It's as if they *should* be accomplished skiers.

Having to get better at skiing, *having* to be perfect, or *having* to please someone else are all counterproductive to learning and performance. This kind of self-generated pressure disrupts your just-right state for skiing well. Pressure generates muscle tension that interferes with maintaining balance and making smooth, controlled, rhythmical turns.

If you find that you're feeling pressure to ski beyond your level of competence, ask yourself what would happen if you didn't. Would you feel you were letting someone else down—your coach, your family, or your friends? Would letting them down make you feel bad?

If the answer is yes, it's quite likely that you're taking unrealistic responsibility for how others feel, and getting your own sense of satisfaction from their approval instead of from yourself. This means that you're unnecessarily dependent on others for feeling good about how you ski. You're playing a dependent mind game instead of taking full responsibility for your own actions and feelings. In other words, you're operating in your mind *as if* you were out there for someone else when actually you're not.

Let's face it: You don't ski—or do anything else, for that matter—solely for another person. *Everything you do is for yourself.* Even when you do something to please someone else, you do it because *you* get something in return— enjoyment from being on the mountain, love, recognition, money, whatever—or you do what you do to avoid something, such as criticism or punishment.

What else might happen if you didn't ski at a higher level? Would you feel embarrassed? Would you feel inadequate as a person? Would you feel dissatisfied with yourself? If your answer to these questions is yes, then your chances of feeling good about yourself are dim.

The true measure of the worth of your skiing ability and yourself is how you feel about your own efforts. If you believe you really applied yourself, irrespective of how great a skier you are, that's all anyone can ask. It's natural to feel disappointment over poor performance. However, feeling embarrassed with how you ski implies a low sense of self-esteem because you allow others to determine your self-worth.

Really wanting to ski well creates a paradox. If you try too hard—if you feel *compelled* to excel—you'll generate pressure that usually results in poor performance. If you minimize becoming an expert and tell yourself just to enjoy skiing, it's highly likely that you'll ski well because your just-right feeling is more apt to be present.

"Shouldniks"

It's easy to spot dependent, compulsive people who put tremendous pressure on themselves to excel. Just listen to their language. They use phrases containing "need to," "must," "got to," "have to," or "should": "I've *got to* practice my stem christies"; "I *should* get through the latter gates faster"; "I *should* have made my turns closer to the fall line"; or "I've *got to* plant my poles sooner." When mistakes on the hill are made, I'll bet many of them arise from being what I call a "shouldnik."

There's a very simple way to eliminate the internal mind game that creates such pressure. It merely involves substituting the phrase "I *want* to do X because . . ." for the words "I *must* (or *should*) do X." When you say "want" with conviction, followed by a reason, you take full responsibility for your wishes and actions. As a result, you'll release a source of energy and motivation to accomplish X. Furthermore, you might realize that you're incapable of doing X, or don't want to do it at all.

Here's an assignment. Make sure you follow it exactly! If you already feel pressure to comply with my command, you'll know that you have a tendency to be a "shouldnik." This exercise will help you overcome it. For the next two weeks, become acutely aware of every time you say "I should" or its equivalent. When you consciously hear it, pay careful attention to how you feel inside—your bodily sensations—just after you admonish yourself. Then substitute the word "want" for "should" and pay attention again to the physical sensations in your body. Compare the two kinds of sensations and notice the difference between them.

Do an exercise with me now. Say to yourself with conviction, "I should [insert something you've been putting off, such as practicing your short-radius turns, working on your pole plants, cutting the grass, balancing the checkbook, washing windows, writing to so-and-so]." What does it feel like in your body when you say this? Make a mental note of the physical feelings.

Now say to yourself, "I *want* to [insert what you said you should do]," paying close attention again to the bodily sensations that are generated as you think about doing it.

Are the "want" feelings different from the "should" feelings? Do you still want to do it? Are you more determined than before to do it? Do you want to get someone else to do it for you? Or do you want to scrap the whole idea?

I can almost guarantee that if you do this exercise faithfully for two full weeks—substituting "want" for every time you say "should"—you'll feel much different about yourself and your life. If you feel that you *should* complete this assignment, ask yourself if you really want to. It's important that you do it out of desire, not compulsion.

Perfectionism

Frequently "shouldniks" are perfectionists. Perfectionists are people who leave no stone unturned to make whatever they do absolutely perfect, without flaw. They are relentless. Please don't misunderstand me. Doing things superbly and paying attention to detail are very important. The point I want to make about perfectionism is that it's the compulsion that things *must* be just so that generates the pressure in yourself to perform beyond *anyone's* capability, let alone your own.

Instead of cursing yourself under your breath when you fall or take an extra-wide turn at a gate, you have another choice of behavior. If the mistake is the result of carelessness, then obviously you're capable of skiing properly. To scold yourself and dwell on the mistake in your mind is counterproductive. First, you generate tension in your muscles that interferes with skiing smoothly. Second, you etch in your nerves and muscles a program to repeat the mistake. And third, you're wasting time and energy.

You have at least one other choice when you make a

careless mistake. Merely say to yourself, "I can make that turn [or whatever]." Picture executing the maneuver correctly in your mind and feeling in your muscles what it's like to ski properly. On the next run, work on correcting the goof. Thinking about the mistake, instead of the correction, grooves the mental program of making the mistake; and you will, time after time.

Establishing Desired Outcomes

Since you can't ski perfectly, what do you want to achieve on the hill? Part of the metaskills approach is to use a systematic way of deciding what's worth achieving and how you can get it with various techniques. This is accomplished by following some basic principles.

Principle of Positivity

Whenever skiers come to me for help, my first question is, "What do you want to accomplish?" Invariably they begin by telling me what's the matter with their ability and what they don't want. Since this approach is usually but not always self-defeating, I play a mind game with them. Let's try an experiment right now to illustrate a very important point that could make your skiing much better with very little work.

In about ten seconds I'm going to tell you to do something. At that time pay attention to what you experience—what you see and hear in your mind, and what you feel in your muscles and other parts of your body. Get ready to follow my instructions. Here goes: Don't be aware of your breathing right now.

What happened? If you're a normal human being, you automatically paid attention to your breathing. Perhaps you felt the rise and fall of your chest and the movement of your abdomen as you inhaled and exhaled. Perhaps you heard the sound of air in your nostrils. If not, check again to see if you're still alive. If so, how come you became aware of your breathing when I told you *not* to?

To understand my direction *not* to pay attention to your breathing, you *had* to turn your mind to the act of breathing. The reason you couldn't *not* become aware of your breathing is the fact that language, the nervous system, and the muscles are "wired" together. Words such as "not" and "don't" are totally ignored. In other words, the nervous system knows no negation.

If you say to yourself, "Don't lean back into the hill," you will access, consciously or unconsciously, a memory of leaning back and probably falling. You couldn't understand my command otherwise. The neural pathways between your brain and the muscles that control leaning into the hill will be activated automatically by my language, probably without your awareness of it.

Of course, you could override this negative command by consciously rehearsing proper balance and control in your mind. There are many people who consistently process information, consciously or unconsciously, by bringing counterexamples—opposites—to mind. Some of these people first think about what they don't want—leaning into the hill—and then shift automatically to thinking about what they do want. Others first think about how they want to ski, yet unconsciously shift to thinking about how they don't want to. This form of unconscious thinking can be devastating to completing a successful run if you're not aware of it.

As you think about your skiing ability right now, consider what you want to be able to do. If you find yourself saying something like "I don't want to make any wide-radius turns," just turn it around and say, "I want to ski crisp, short-radius turns." Do you feel different inside when you say this?

Principle of Specificity

The more you know precisely what you want to accomplish or do, the easier it will be to get it. You could say, "I want to be able consistently to keep my weight forward with my hands up." This statement can be further specified to include a more precise definition of "consistently," such as skiing in this manner during eight of ten runs.

The statement can be refined still further by identifying, in sensory-specific terms, what you would see, hear, and feel as you execute the ten runs well. For example, you might want to feel your boots touch your shins; you might want to see your hands directly in front of your shoulders; you might want to adjust your grip on the poles; you might want to hear a certain kind of "schuss" as you turn; or you might want to visualize a certain kind of line that you want to follow down the hill.

Sometimes it's hard to pinpoint exactly what you want to change so your skiing improves. This is especially true for expert skiers because everything is so grooved. The clue to your corrections is often reflected in language, especially the verbs, adverbs, and adjectives used to describe a problem.

Once when I was working with a skier, she said to me, "My turns don't *feel rhythmical*." This statement suggested that there were both kinesthetic (*feel*) and auditory (*rhythmical*) components to her turning analysis.

"Which muscles specifically don't *feel* right, and what kind of *sound* would you like to go along with your turns?" I asked.

She looked down at the snow for a moment. Then she hummed to herself quietly as she leaned from side to side. "Oh, now I know what it is," she answered. "I'm hurrying my release out of each turn. I'm not riding my edges long enough. I wasn't humming a tune the way I usually do when I ski well. Let me try another run with a song in mind."

She hummed to herself throughout the next run and reported, "Now my turns feel rhythmical, the way I want them to."

My work with her was finished. I had just pointed her in the direction of her own knowledge, revealed in her language. Metaskills techniques do exactly that.

The Backup Process

There's another way to uncover unknown elements of your skiing maneuvers in need of refinement. It's the Backup Process, described on page 118. As you may recall, it consists of mentally rehearsing your *anticipated* performance in a *forthcoming* race. By skiing an entire racecourse in your mind, you can uncover the most difficult parts of it by noticing the blurred images, dissonant sounds, and uncomfortable feelings that occur at certain sections of the course. Practicing on these sections of the course can then become the basis for establishing your immediate desired outcome because you'll find out precisely what you want to correct.

Principle of Ecology

Everything with which human beings interact has a definite impact on their well-being. There is an interdependence among our beliefs, behaviors, expectations, nutrition, health, personal relationships, and the environment. Change any one of these elements and it could have a powerful effect on some or all of the others.

Recall, for example, what Jessica discovered about her skiing injury. At first she felt compelled to get back on skis. She felt haunted by it and lost confidence in herself. Now she's beginning to believe that it might not be ecological for her to continue skiing. A subsequent injury could result in permanent damage to her knee, followed by extensive reconstructive surgery. When she gave full attention to her belief and changed it, she felt "cleansed."

You, too, can determine the ecological soundness of any desired outcome by answering two sets of important questions:

- What will achieving a particular outcome do for you? What will be the outcomes of that outcome?
- What's the worst that could happen if you achieve your outcome? Can you think of any reason why achieving it would *not* be in your best interests?

By answering these questions you will identify the potential positive and negative effects of achieving an outcome *before* you even pursue it. By doing this you will either become more strongly motivated to achieve it, or you'll realize that its achievement may not be worth the effort. In both cases you'll save time and energy, and avoid potential disappointment and disruption in your life.

Here are the steps to follow to establish ecologically

sound outcomes. Knowing them, you'll be ready to select appropriate metaskills techniques to achieve them.

ESTABLISHING DESIRED OUTCOMES

1. Identify a particular maneuver (a desired outcome) that you want to learn or improve. Do this by using the Backup Process on page 118, or consult with your ski instructor.

2. State your desired outcome in positive terms. Indicate what you want, not what you don't want (principle of positivity).

3. Identify and evaluate the potential positive and negative consequences of achieving a desired outcome *before* you pursue it. If your evaluation is positive, continue to the next step. If not, go back to Step 1 and identify another outcome (principle of ecology).

4. Define your desired outcome in precise sensory terms, knowing what you will see, hear, and feel when your outcome has been achieved (principle of specificity).

Going for It

Achieving positive, ecologically sound outcomes through metaskills techniques can be simple if you go for them one at a time. Just pay attention to only one or two elements of each maneuver until each becomes automatic—that is, until it becomes regulated by your unconscious mind. Work with only one metaskills technique at a time. Gradually you'll learn to run your brain and control your moods so you can eventually ski all kinds of terrain under different snow and weather conditions.

But which metaskills techniques are most appropriate for your specific desired outcomes? In Appendix B I have prepared an outline with page references that briefly describes the purposes of each technique and which ones can be used to achieve various desired outcomes. It serves as a quick reference to help you select the technique most appropriate for a particular outcome you have in mind. Frequently more than one technique can be used to achieve a desired outcome, and most techniques can be applied to achieve a number of different outcomes.

I suggest that you use my techniques experimentally. By that I mean fully commit yourself to following the steps of each technique exactly as presented. While doing this, notice what happens to the quality of your skiing. When one technique doesn't work after a couple of applications, use another.

After each practice session, ask yourself the question "What did I learn?," regardless of the results. I really want you to think deeply about what you learn about yourself— your moods, the way you think, the things you value, and the way you feel about life and skiing. Then truly honor what you've discovered about your inner self. Once you know and honor yourself, you can let your unconscious mind do all the work on the hill while your conscious mind enjoys the skiing, the scenery, and your companions.

When you truly honor yourself, you'll be free of internal conflicts that sap your energy and interfere with safe and satisfying skiing. Without self-knowledge and acceptance, you'll be skiing against yourself, interfering with the work of the unconscious mind that automatically regulates good skiing performance.

Appendix A

Sensory Awareness

This appendix contains two parts: (1) a series of questions that identify how people internally represent their sensory experience, and (2) exercises designed to strengthen sensory awareness.

Representation of Sensory Experience

The questions that follow are modifications of what Richard Bandler and Will MacDonald presented in their book *An Insider's Guide to Sub-Modalities*. Submodalities are classified according to each of the three main channels of awareness crucial for regulating athletic skills: vision, audition (sound), and kinesthesia (feeling). The senses of smell and taste are of little consequence in sports.

These questions can serve as a handy reference when you're practicing several metaskills techniques: the Sherlock Holmes Exercise, just-right anchors, Discovering Differences, and self-hypnosis. Whenever the instructions for any of these techniques tell you to change how you see, hear, and feel "on the inside" or in your mind, the following questions can help you do just that.

Vision

Brightness: Are the images brighter than normal, with lots of light, or are they dark? Are some images brighter than others?

Color: Are the images in color or black and white? Is there a full spectrum of color, or is there a dominance of one or more colors?

Contrast: Is there a sharp contrast in the objects and colors, or are they subdued or washed out?

Focus: Are the images sharply focused or fuzzy?

Distance: Are you looking at the image as if zoomed in, or do you have a wide-angle view? How wide is the angle?

Location: Where is your mental screen? Is it within your head? Is it outside of you—to the front, side, rear, down, up? How far away is it (in feet and inches)? Does the screen on which the image is projected move? If so, in what direction?

Size: How big is the screen (approximately, in inches or feet)? Does the size change?

Shape: Is the screen round, square, triangular, rectangular?

Border: Does the screen have a frame or a border? Describe the size and design of the border.

Viewpoint: Are you seeing yourself in the picture as if you were a spectator, or are you seeing what you would normally see if you were actually there? From what direction are you looking at yourself—from the side (right or left), back, front, above, at an angle? Is your internal screen tilted at an angle from front to back or from side to side? Does the screen seem to wrap around you, or is it flat and two-dimensional?

Motion: Is the image a still picture, or are you watching a movie? Is there a series of images, like slides flashing on the screen one by one? Do you see multiple still pictures one at a time or all at once? If you're seeing a movie, is it like a loop film, running over and over again? How fast are the motion pictures moving—at normal speed, slower than normal, or faster than normal?

Number: How many screens are there? How many images are there on each screen? Are the images separate? Are they arranged side by side or vertically? Are some superimposed on others?

Audition (Hearing)

Volume: How loud is the sound? Is it normal, above normal, or below normal?

Duration: Does the sound persist continuously, or is it intermittent?

Pitch: Are the sounds high- or low-pitched?

Tone: Are the sounds thin, full, rich, grating, harsh, pleasant, resonant?

Melody: Is the sound harmonious, discordant, monotonous?

Tempo: Is the beat fast or slow?

Rhythm: Is the rhythm syncopated or even-cadenced?

Location: Where, specifically, is the source of the sound? At a particular point within your body? Outside your body?

Direction: In what direction does the sound flow? Does it flow from inside out, outside in, upward, downward? Is the sound stereophonic, or do you hear it from only one direction?

Background: Are there background noises? If so, ask the questions above.

Kinesthesia (Feeling)

It's important to distinguish the feelings that signify an emotional state as contrasted with the feelings of skillful movement performance. Each of the following categories applies to both skillful performance and emotional states.

Location: Where, specifically, in your body do you feel the sensations? Does the feeling remain in one place, or does it spread? Is the feeling localized, or spread throughout your body? Is there a difference in feelings on each side of your body? Is there a difference in feelings in the upper half as contrasted with the lower half of your body?

Duration: Do the feelings persist, or are they intermittent?

Characterization: How would you describe the quality of the feelings? Warm/cold? Relaxed/tense? Heavy/light? Extended/contracted? Even/pulsating? Strong/weak? Pleasant/uncomfortable?

Movement: How would you describe the nature of your movements? Strong/weak? Coordinated/disjointed? Gentle/ballistic? Smooth/jerky? Flexible/stiff or limited? Relaxed/tense? Slow/quick? Balanced/unbalanced?

Intensity: How strong are the sensations? What is the degree of strength, power, balance, relaxation, flexibility, smoothness, warmth, lightness, coordination in relation to normal?

Sensory Awareness Exercises

Few people process visual, auditory, and kinesthetic information equally well. Most of us are strong in the use of one or two senses and weak in others. The exercises that follow are designed to strengthen your weaker senses. Most of the exercises can be done at any time, anywhere—while on an easy slope, riding to work, listening to a boring lecture, showering, cutting the grass, or riding on the lift.

These exercises are merely examples of a few ways to improve your sensory awareness; use your ingenuity to create others.

Crossover Training

Crossover training is a series of exercises that make use of the natural, inborn synesthesia "wiring" in your brain and nervous system. They capitalize on the strength of your most sensitive sensory channel as a way to build up your sensitivity in other channels.

Crossover from Hearing to Other Channels
Hear a bird sing and make a *picture* of a bird in your mind. *Hear* an automobile horn and *feel* the vibrations of the horn's sound in some part of your body. In your mind, *hear* the schuss of your skis and *feel* yourself turning on your skis.

Crossover from Feeling to Other Channels
When you *feel* anger, see a *color*. Convert a painful *feeling* into the *sound* "Ouch!" While *feeling* medium-radius turns, generate in your mind's eye an *image* of skiing down a specific trail.

Crossover from Seeing to Other Channels

Make an internal *image* of a fire engine and *hear* its siren in your mind. Make a picture in your mind of a pleasant *scene* and pay attention to where in your body you have a pleasant *feeling*. *Observe* someone lifting something heavy and *feel* the strain of the muscular effort involved in your own muscles. Create an internal *image* of a skier turning and *hear* in your mind the sound of his skis on the snow.

Visual Imagery

Internal visual imagery is central to skiing well. It prepares you mentally for each maneuver and helps you analyze and correct your form. The following exercises are designed to increase your internal visual skills.

Making Meta Pictures

A meta picture is an internal image in which you see yourself as if you were looking through someone else's eyes, like watching yourself skiing on videotape. This is an important imagery skill because it helps you evaluate your own skiing movements.

- Seated comfortably in a chair, wiggle your toes, and feel your feet on the floor. Now make a picture of only your feet. Next, move your lower leg and make a picture of it from the knee down; connect that picture to the one of your feet. Next, contract your thigh muscles, move your leg, and make a picture of your thigh; connect that picture to the previous picture of your lower legs and feet. Continue until you have connected your entire body. Don't forget your head.

By this time you should have a complete meta picture of yourself.

- Practice making meta pictures of yourself while skiing on different terrain. Become very sensitive to what each part of your body is doing as you ski.
- Watch a portion of a videotaped recording of, for example, a professional skier making short-radius turns. Stop the tape, close your eyes, and visually reproduce the turns in your mind. Replay the videotape to determine the accuracy of your self-generated, internal movie. Adjust your internal images until they match the turns on the videoscreen.

Making Superimposed Pictures and Multiple Images

- Project onto the surface of an actual trail an imaginary moving picture of yourself skiing.
- On an imaginary screen within your head, project several slide pictures of yourself turning to the right and left. Use these mental slides as a guide for practicing your turns.
- Make a movie of a particular skiing maneuver in your mind's eye; vary its brightness, sharpness, size, color, and focus. Notice what effect these variations have on the quality of the imaginary maneuver.

Auditory Awareness

I'm sure you realize that there are times during a run down the hill when you talk to yourself or hear the voices of others in your mind telling you what to do or what not to do. They can be useful when they're in your control or a hindrance when they're not. Most of the time internal sound interferes with skiing well. Similarly, external noises can be distracting when you're skiing unless you know how to tune them out or use them constructively. The following are exercises to increase your sensitivity to sounds; use them in your mind to improve your skiing ability.

External Auditory

- Listen to the voice of someone on the radio or on television; turn off the sound and mimic the tone, volume, and syntax of the voice; turn the sound back on and compare the sound of your own voice with the one you heard. Repeat this process until you can mimic the voice as well as possible.
- Mimic as well as you can the sounds of animals as you hear them—a bird singing, for example, or a dog barking.
- Listen intently to a distracting sound while skiing on an easy hill. Notice the quality of your skiing. Now pretend the distracting sound is entering your muscles, creating energy in your body and making your skiing stronger. Notice the quality of your turns. Are they better than normal?

Internal Auditory

- Modify the volume and tone of your own or someone else's voice that you hear inside your head. Vary the nature of the internal voice from loud, harsh, and critical to soft, pleasant, and supportive. Notice how your bodily sensations vary with the change in tone and volume.

- When you hear an internal critical voice, substitute pleasant music. Notice any change in body tension.

- Deliberately talk to yourself *while* skiing a section of an easy hill and notice the quality of your performance. Then quiet your mind, ski another section, and notice the quality of that performance. Is there a difference?

- Immediately after skiing a section of any easy trail, deliberately criticize yourself harshly in your mind, and notice the amount of tension in your body. Then stop criticizing yourself and ski another section. Notice the quality of your skiing the second section. Was the second section better or worse than the first? If better, perhaps you were too tense during the first section; if worse, perhaps you became too relaxed.

- Now change the internal critical voice to a calm, supportive one, giving yourself positive instructions on skiing well. How much physical tension do you feel when you change the tone of your internal voice from critical to supportive?

Kinesthetic Awareness

Contrary to logical expectations, I have found that many athletes are largely unaware of their bodily sensations. Some skiers are insensitive to the specific muscle tensions involved in making a turn. Others are unaware of the bodily sensations linked to their emotional states when they are skiing difficult sections of a hill. Lacking these sensitivities, skiers are missing important information that could improve their ability immensely. For example, if you're unaware of the amount of tension in your hands, wrists, and forearms, it will be difficult to control a pole plant. The following exercises are designed to refine your awareness of physical tensions and emotion because they have a direct bearing on the smoothness and rhythm of various skiing maneuvers.

Body Scanning

Several times a day, stop doing whatever you are doing and pay attention to the amount of tension/relaxation and warmth/coolness that exist in various parts of your body —head, neck, shoulders, arms, wrists, hands, fingers, chest, abdomen, back, hips, thighs, knees, calves, ankles, feet, and toes.

Physical Sensations Related to Turning

- Increase and decrease the amount of tension in your legs and ankles as you make a series of turns; the tension should vary from very loose to very tight. Notice the quality of your turns.
- Immediately after making a fine run, reproduce it in your mind and become aware of the amount of tension you feel in your legs, shoulders, hands, wrists, and forearms. Do the same thing after skiing poorly. Determine the differences in muscle tension when skiing well and when skiing poorly.

Emotional Awareness

You probably know that emotions affect muscle tension and therefore are linked closely to the way you ski. Emotional states can either facilitate or disrupt your performance. Anger at yourself after falling or after a poor turn usually increases muscle tension in your entire body.

Muscle tension causes inflexibility and affects the tempo of your turns. In both cases the quality of your performance is affected. The following exercises will help you increase your emotional awareness.

- Each time you become aware of a strong emotion, scan your body to identify the specific physical sensations that accompany it. For example, clenched fists suggest anger, butterflies in the stomach usually mean fear, and tightness in the leg muscles could mean frustration. Notice the most intense sensations related to each emotional state and how that tension affects the quality of your skiing.
- Experiment with increasing and then decreasing tension in the muscles associated with a particular emotion identified in the previous exercise. Is there any change in your emotional state? Again notice how it affects your skiing.
- When an emotion—for instance, fear, frustration, or worry—becomes too strong while skiing, stop in a safe place out of the way of traffic; decrease the tension in the muscles associated with the emotion; look upward and make an internal image of a pleasant scene. Is there a reduction in emotional intensity? Does your skiing improve?

Appendix B

Guide to Selecting Metaskills Techniques

This appendix is a ready reference and guide to selecting appropriate metaskills techniques to achieve various desired outcomes. It contains two parts: (1) an alphabetical listing of the techniques and the purposes they serve, and (2) an alphabetical listing of common desired outcomes and the techniques that can be used to achieve them.

For detailed information about each technique, refer to the pages in parentheses. You may also use the index to locate anecdotes related to the various techniques.

Techniques and the Purposes They Serve

Anchoring (p. 52)

Control anxiety.
Improve concentration.
Increase confidence.

Increase consistency.
Improve memory.
Stabilize a state of consciousness.
Change a state of consciousness quickly.
Apply inner resources.
Facilitate unconscious control of performance.

Backup Process (p. 119)

Identify outcomes.
Analyze performance.
Plan practice sessions.
Prepare for races.

Body Scanning (p. 202)

Increase awareness of emotional states.
Analyze performance.
Facilitate use of Discovering Difference.
Facilitate anchoring.
Facilitate pain control.

"Breakthrough" (p. 84)

Overcome fear and anxiety.
Increase confidence.
Increase consistency.

Challenge Process (p. 95)

Build confidence.
Overcome anxiety, doubt, and fear.
Prepare to ski a difficult trail.

Colored-Image Anchor (p. 102)

Increase concentration.
Increase confidence.

Maintain consistency.
Stabilize emotional state.

Competitive-State Anchor (p. 71)

Control anxiety.
Increase concentration.
Increase confidence.
Increase consistency.
Prepare for a forthcoming race.

Confidence Anchor (p. 107)

Build confidence.
Maintain confidence.

Counting Process (p. 114)

Improve coordination and timing.
Regulate turning tempo.

Crossover Training (p. 197)

Improve capacity to make internal images.
Increase sensitivity to bodily sensations.
Increase sensitivity to sound.
Improve capacity to become aware of internal
    dialogue.
Increase ability to use metaskills techniques.

Discovering Difference (p. 122)

Reduce confusion.
Increase consistency.
Analyze performance.

Establishing Desired Outcomes (p. 184)

Identify worthwhile outcomes.
Specify precisely what you want to accomplish.
Develop positive outlook.
Improve practice sessions.

"Flash" (p. 86)

Control anxiety.
Increase concentration.
Clear mind of unwanted thoughts.
Change state.

Get-It-Back Process (p. 132)

Relearn maneuvers.

Get-It Process (p. 129)

Learn new maneuvers.

Holographic Viewing (p. 132)

Analyze performance.
Acquire new skills.

Inside Out (p. 161)

Reduce or eliminate pain.

M & M Process (p. 111)

Increase consistency.
Improve coordination and timing.
Change emotional state.
Stabilize emotional state.
Establish and maintain turning tempo.

Metaphors (p. 131)

Improve concentration.
Maintain consistency.
Facilitate healing.
Create optimal performance state.

Meta Pictures (p. 198)

Control anxiety.
Reduce pain.
Reduce intensity of uncomfortable feelings.
Analyze performance.
Gain a new perspective.

Metaskills Healing (p. 177)

Speed up healing.
Heal without surgery or medication.

Multiple Images (p. 199)

Improve consistency.
Analyze performance.
Facilitate route planning.

Off-Ramp Technique (p. 114)

Regulate turning tempo.
Improve coordination and timing.

Personal Power Anchor (p. 75)

Overcome anxiety and fear.
Build confidence.
Tap resources of excellence and effectiveness.

Reframing (p. 173)

Control anxiety.
Modify beliefs and values.
Facilitate healing.
Create new perspective.

Resource Anchor (p. 68)

Increase confidence.
Increase consistency.

Route Planning (p. 59)

Increase confidence.
Increase safety.
Regulate speed.

Self-Hypnosis (Betty Erickson Technique) (p. 141)

Build confidence.
Maintain concentration.
Facilitate healing.
Create just-right state.
Access mental strategies.
Control pain.
Analyze performance.
Develop relaxed state.
Access long-forgotten experiences.
Distort perception of time.
Build trust in the unconscious mind.
Change unwanted habit patterns.

Sherlock Holmes Exercise (p. 31)

Understand mental processing.
Analyze performance.

Identify elements of mental strategies.
Improve memory.
Identify internal resources from past experiences.
Recall past performances.
Identify important performance keys.
Identify just-right states.
Facilitate getting into an altered state.

"Shouldnik" (p. 181)

Control anxiety.
Reduce compulsive behavior.
Identify worthwhile desired outcomes.

"Stop" (p. 86)

Control anxiety.
Clear mind of unwanted thoughts.

Trauma Reduction (p. 168)

Control anxiety.
Decrease mental anguish.
Increase confidence.
Reframe the meaning of a traumatic experience.
Recall forgotten details of traumatic experience.
Change perspective.

Video Mimicry (p. 153)

Increase consistency.
Analyze performance.
Learn new maneuvers.

Visual Imagery (p. 198)

Analyze performance.
Increase sensory acuity.
Facilitate use of most metaskills techniques.

"Zoom" (p. 60)

Increase confidence.
Analyze performance.
Map route down the hill.
Increase safety.

Desired Outcomes and the Techniques to Use

The following is a list of typical desired outcomes and the metaskills techniques that can be used to achieve them.

Anxiety Control

Anchoring
"Breakthrough"
Challenge Process
Colored-Image Anchor
Competitive-State Anchor
Confidence Anchor
"Flash"
Meta Pictures
Personal Power Anchor
Reframing
Route Planning
Self-Hypnosis
"Shouldnik"
"Stop"
Trauma Reduction

Concentration

Anchoring
Colored-Image Anchor
Discovering Difference
"Flash"
M & M Process
Metaphors
Self-Hypnosis
"Stop"
"Zoom"

Confidence

Anchoring
"Breakthrough"
Challenge Process
Colored-Image Anchor
Competitive-State Anchor
Confidence Anchor
Discovering Difference
Get-It-Back Process
Personal Power Anchor
Reframing
Route Planning
Self-Hypnosis
"Shouldnik"
Trauma Reduction
"Zoom"

Confusion, Reducing

Confidence Anchor
Discovering Difference
Establishing Desired Outcomes

"Flash"
Personal Power Anchor
Reframing
"Shouldnik"
"Stop"
Trauma Reduction

Consistency of Performance

Colored-Image Anchor
Competitive-State Anchor
Confidence Anchor
Discovering Difference
Meta Pictures
Video Mimicry

Healing

Metaskills Healing
Reframing
Self-Hypnosis
Trauma Reduction

Learning New Maneuvers

Get-It Process
Holographic Viewing
Meta Pictures
Video Mimicry

Outcomes, Determining

Backup Process
Challenge Process
Establishing Desired Outcomes
"Shouldnik"

Pain Control

Inside Out
Meta Pictures
Self-Hypnosis
Trauma Reduction

Performance Analysis

Backup Process
Body Scanning
Discovering Difference
Get-It Process
Get-It-Back Process
Holographic Viewing
Meta Pictures
Multiple Images
Self-Hypnosis
Sherlock Holmes Exercise
Video Mimicry
Visual Imagery

Race Preparation

Backup Process
Competitive-State Anchor
Confidence Anchor
Discovering Difference
Route Planning
Self-Hypnosis
Sherlock Holmes Exercise
Video Mimicry
"Zoom"

Stabilize State

Colored-Image Anchor
Competitive-State Anchor
M & M Process
Metaphors
Self-Hypnosis

State Change

"Breakthrough"
Challenge Process
Competitive-State Anchor
Discovering Difference
"Flash"
M & M Process
Meta Pictures
Personal Power Anchor
Self-Hypnosis
Sherlock Holmes Exercise
Trauma Reduction

Turning Tempo

Counting Process
Discovering Difference
Get-It Process
M & M Process
Metaphors
Off-Ramp Technique
Self-Hypnosis
Video Mimicry

Selected References: Neuro-Linguistic Programming

Andreas, Connirae, and Steve Andreas. *Heart of the Mind.* Moab, Utah: Real People Press, 1989.

Andreas, Steve, and Connirae Andreas. *Change Your Mind —and Keep the Change.* Moab, Utah: Real People Press, 1987.

Bandler, Richard. *Magic in Action.* Cupertino, Calif.: Meta Publications, 1984.

———. *Using Your Brain—For a Change.* Moab, Utah: Real People Press, 1985.

Bandler, Richard, and John Grinder. *The Structure of Magic,* Vol. 1. Palo Alto, Calif.: Science and Behavior Books, 1975.

———. *Frogs into Princes.* Moab, Utah: Real People Press, 1979.

————. *Reframing: Neuro-Linguistic Programming and the Transformation of Meaning.* Moab, Utah: Real People Press, 1982.

Bandler, Richard, and Will MacDonald. *An Insider's Guide to Sub-Modalities.* Cupertino, Calif.: Meta Publications, 1988.

Cameron-Bandler, Leslie. *Solutions.* San Rafael, Calif.: Future Pace, 1985.

Dilts, Robert; *Changing Belief Systems with NLP.* Cupertino, Calif.: Meta Publications, 1990.

Dilts, Robert; Tim Hallbom, and Suzi Smith. *Beliefs: Pathways to Health & Well-Being.* Portland, Ore.: Metamorphous Press, 1990.

Dilts, Robert B., et al. *Neuro-Linguistic Programming,* Vol. 1. Cupertino, Calif.: Meta Publications, 1980.

Grinder, John, and Richard Bandler. *The Structure of Magic,* Vol. 2. Palo Alto, Calif.: Science and Behavior Books, 1976.

Laborde, Genie Z. *Influencing with Integrity: Management Skills for Communication and Negotiation.* Palo Alto, Calif.: Science and Behavior Books, 1984.

————. *Fine Tune Your Brain.* Palo Alto, Calif.: Syntony Publishing, 1988.

Mackenzie, Marlin M., with Ken Denlinger. *Golf: The Mind Game.* New York: Dell Publishing, 1990.

————. *Tennis: The Mind Game.* New York: Dell Publishing, 1991.

McMaster, Michael, and John Grinder. *Precision: A New Approach to Communication.* Beverly Hills, Calif.: Precision Models, 1980.

Robbins, Anthony. *Unlimited Power.* New York: Simon & Schuster, 1986.

Index